Making Data Visual
A Practical Guide to Using Visualization for Insight

Danyel Fisher and Miriah Meyer

Beijing · Boston · Farnham · Sebastopol · Tokyo

Making Data Visual

by Danyel Fisher and Miriah Meyer

Copyright © 2018 Miriah Meyer, Microsoft. All rights reserved.

Printed in the United States of America.

Published by O'Reilly Media, Inc., 1005 Gravenstein Highway North, Sebastopol, CA 95472.

O'Reilly books may be purchased for educational, business, or sales promotional use. Online editions are also available for most titles (*http://oreilly.com/safari*). For more information, contact our corporate/institutional sales department: 800-998-9938 or *corporate@oreilly.com*.

Editor: Rachel Roumeliotis	**Interior Designer:** David Futato
Production Editor: Justin Billing	**Cover Designer:** Karen Montgomery
Copyeditor: Rachel Head	**Illustrator:** Rebecca Demarest
Proofreader: Gillian McGarvey	**Additional illustrations:** Dominik Moritz
Indexer: Ellen Troutman-Zaig	and Kanit "Ham" Wongsuphasawat

January 2018:   First Edition

Revision History for the First Edition
2017-12-19:   First Release

See *http://bit.ly/making-data-visual* for release details.

The O'Reilly logo is a registered trademark of O'Reilly Media, Inc. *Making Data Visual*, the cover image, and related trade dress are trademarks of O'Reilly Media, Inc.

978-1-491-92846-2

[LSI]

Table of Contents

Preface

Visualization is a vital tool for understanding and sharing insights around data. The right visualization can help express a core idea or open a space to examination; it can get the world talking about a dataset or sharing an insight Figure P-1.

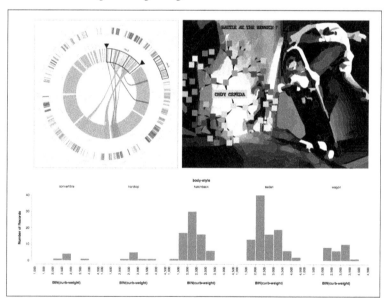

Figure P-1. Visualizations can take many forms, from views that support exploratory analysis (top left), to those that provide quick overviews in a dashboard (bottom), to an infographic about popular topics (top right).

Visualizations provide a direct and tangible representation of data. They allow people to confirm hypotheses and gain insights. When incorporated into the data analysis process early and often, visualizations can even fundamentally alter the questions that someone is asking.

Creating effective visualizations is hard. Not because a dataset requires an exotic and bespoke visual representation—for many problems, standard statistical charts will suffice. And not because creating a visualization requires coding expertise in an unfamiliar programming language—off-the-shelf tools like Excel (*https://products.office.com/en-us/excel*), Tableau (*https://www.tableau.com/*), and R (*https://www.r-project.org/*) are ample enough to suffice.

Rather, creating effective visualizations is difficult because the problems that are best addressed by visualization are often complex and ill-formed. The task of figuring out *what attributes* of a dataset are important is often conflated with figuring out *what type of visualization* to use. Picking a chart type to represent specific attributes in a dataset is comparatively easy. Deciding on which data attributes will help answer a question, however, is a complex, poorly defined, and user-driven process that can require several rounds of visualization and exploration to resolve. In this book, we focus on the process of going from high-level questions to well-defined data analysis tasks, and on how to incorporate visualizations along the way to clarify understanding and gain insights.

Who Is This Book For?

This book is for people who have access to data and, perhaps, a suite of computational tools but who are less than sure how to turn that data into visual insights. We find that many data science books assume that you can figure out how to visualize the data once collected, and visualization books assume that you already have a well-defined question, ready to be visualized. If, like us, you would like to address these assumptions, then this book is for you.

This book does not cover how to clean and manage data in detail or how to write visualization code. There are already great books on these topics (and, when relevant, we point to some of them). Rather, this book speaks to why those processes are important. Similarly, this book does not address how to choose a beautiful colormap or select a typeface. Instead, we lay out a framework for how to think about data given the possibilities and constraints of visual exploration. Our goal is to show how to effectively use visualizations to make sense of data.

Who Are We?

The authors of this book have a combined three decades of experience in making sense of data through designing and using visualizations. We have worked with data from a broad range of fields: biology and urban transportation, business intelligence and scientific visualization, debugging code and building maps. We have worked with analysts from a variety of organizations, from small, academic science labs to teams of data analysts embedded in large companies. Some of the projects we have worked on have resulted in sophisticated, bespoke visualization systems designed collaboratively with domain specialists, and at other times we have pointed people to off-the-shelf visualization tools after a few conversations. We have taught university classes in visualization and have given lectures and tutorials. All in all, we have visualized hundreds of datasets.

We have found that our knowledge about visualization techniques, solutions, and systems shapes the way that we think and reason about data. Visualization is fundamentally about presenting data in a way that elicits human reasoning, makes room for individual interpretations, and supports exploration. We help our collaborators make their questions and data reflect these values. The process we lay out in this book describes our method for doing this.

Overview of Chapters

Chapter 1 illustrates the process of making sense with visualizations through a quick example, exposing the role that a visual representation can play in data discovery.

Chapter 2 starts to get into details. It discusses a mechanism to help narrow a question from a broad task into something that can be addressed with an iterative visualization process. For example, the broad question "Who are the best movie directors?" does not necessarily suggest a specific visualization—but "Find movie directors who directed top-grossing movies using an IMDB dataset" can lead more directly to an answer by way of a visualization or two. This process creates an *operationalized* question, one that consists of particular tasks that can be directly addressed with data.

This process of narrowing a question down to actionable tasks requires input from multiple stakeholders. Chapter 3 lays out an iterative set of steps for getting to the operationalization, which we call *data counseling*. These steps include finding the right people to talk to, asking effective questions, and rapidly exploring the data through increasingly sophisticated prototypes.

The numerical nitty-gritty of the book follows. Chapter 4 discusses types and relations of data, and defines terms like *dimensions, measures, categorical,* and *quantitative.* Chapter 5 then organizes common visualization types by the tasks they fulfill and the data they use. Then, Chapter 6 explores powerful visualization techniques that use multiple views and interaction to support analysis of large, complex datasets. These three chapters are meant to provide an overview of some of the most effective and commonly used ideas for supporting sensemaking with visualizations, and are framed using the operationalization and data counseling process to help guide decision-making about which visualizations to choose.

With this understanding of getting to insight—from questions to data to visualizations—the remainder of the book illustrates two examples of carrying out these steps. The case study in Chapter 7 describes the creation of a business intelligence dashboard in collaboration with a team of developers and analysts at Microsoft. The one in Chapter 8 draws from science, presenting an example with a team of scientists who work with biological data. These case studies illustrate the flexibility of the process laid out in this book, as well as the diverse types of outcomes that are possible.

This book is accompanied by a companion website (*https://resour ces.oreilly.com/examples/0636920041320*). From this site you can download the code and interactive versions of the visualizations presented in Chapters 5 and 6, as well as other code and supplementary material.

Acknowledgments

Danyel and Miriah would like to thank Danyel's colleagues at Microsoft, including Steven Drucker, Mary Czerwinski, and Sue Dumais, for their enthusiasm and encouragement. We also thank

Miriah's research group, the Visualization Design Lab at the University of Utah, including Alex Lex, for helping the project to evolve and providing feedback on ideas. We are both deeply appreciative of our work organizations for supporting the time and energy required by projects like this one, and for seeing the value in communicating our research broadly. At O'Reilly Media, we thank Mike Loukides for encouraging us to start this work, and Shannon Cutt and Rachel Roumeliotis for guiding it from start to finish.

Portions of this work were presented at the IPAM Workshop on Culture Analytics of 2016, Microsoft Data Insights Summit of 2016, University of Illinois Urbana-Champaign HCI Seminar Series of 2016, University of British Columbia HCI Seminar Series of 2016, Women in Data Science Conference at Stanford University in 2017, and O'Reilly Velocity Conference in 2017. Our thanks to the organizers of those events, and to participants who gave us critical feedback and helped clarify our thoughts.

Early feedback on the operationalization process came from Christian Canton of Microsoft. Michael Twidale and Andrea Thomer, both of UIUC, helped inform the discussion of data counseling with their insights on how reference librarians do their work.

We are grateful to Dominik Mortiz (*https://www.domoritz.de/*) and Kanit "Ham" Wongsuphasawat (*http://kanitw.github.io/*) for putting together the examples used in Chapters 5 and 6. Their work, as well as that of the rest of the Vega-Lite team, is helping shape the future of data visualization. We also thank Alex Bigelow for supplying the skateboading visualization figure in the Preface.

We thank Jacqueline Richards for her review and discussion of the case study in Chapter 7. Similarly, the collaboration with Angela DePace and her group at the Harvard Medical School for the case study in Chapter 8 provided valuable and rich insights into the process of designing visualizations for domain experts. The projects described in both of these chapters were deeply influential in our work practices.

Our technical reviewers, Michael Freeman, Jeff Heer, and Jerry Overton, helped clarify and strengthen the arguments we make.

Finally, Miriah thanks Brian Price for his endless support and encouragement, without which she could never do the things she does.

O'Reilly Safari

 *Safari* (formerly Safari Books Online) is a membership-based training and reference platform for enterprise, government, educators, and individuals.

Members have access to thousands of books, training videos, Learning Paths, interactive tutorials, and curated playlists from over 250 publishers, including O'Reilly Media, Harvard Business Review, Prentice Hall Professional, Addison-Wesley Professional, Microsoft Press, Sams, Que, Peachpit Press, Adobe, Focal Press, Cisco Press, John Wiley & Sons, Syngress, Morgan Kaufmann, IBM Redbooks, Packt, Adobe Press, FT Press, Apress, Manning, New Riders, McGraw-Hill, Jones & Bartlett, and Course Technology, among others.

For more information, please visit *http://oreilly.com/safari*.

How to Contact Us

Please address comments and questions concerning this book to the publisher:

O'Reilly Media, Inc.
1005 Gravenstein Highway North
Sebastopol, CA 95472
800-998-9938 (in the United States or Canada)
707-829-0515 (international or local)
707-829-0104 (fax)

We have a web page for this book, where we list errata, examples, and any additional information. You can access this page at *http://bit.ly/making-data-visual*.

To comment or ask technical questions about this book, send email to *bookquestions@oreilly.com*.

For more information about our books, courses, conferences, and news, see our website at *http://www.oreilly.com*.

Find us on Facebook: *http://facebook.com/oreilly*

Follow us on Twitter: *http://twitter.com/oreillymedia*

Watch us on YouTube: *http://www.youtube.com/oreillymedia*

Getting to an Effective Visualization

Choosing or designing a good visualization is rarely a straightforward process. It is tempting to believe that there is one beautiful visualization that will show all the critical aspects of a dataset. That the *right* visual representation will reveal hidden insights. That a perfect, simple, and elegant visualization—perhaps just a line chart or a well-chosen scatterplot—will show precisely what the important variable was and how it varied in precisely the way to illustrate a critical lesson.

This is often the impression that we, at least, are left with after reading data science case studies. But in our experience, this does not match the reality of visual data analysis. It takes hard work, and trial and error, to get to an insightful visualization. We start by thinking about what we want to know, and we refine fuzzy questions into actionable, concrete tasks. We clean, reshape, and restructure the data into forms that we can put into a visualization. We work around limitations in the data, and we try to understand what the user wants to learn. We have to consider which visual representations to use and what interaction mechanisms to support. Along the way, we find other variables that tell us more about the dataset and that help clarify our thinking. And no single visualization is ever quite able to show all of the important aspects of our data at once— there just are not enough visual encoding channels.

Designing effective visualizations presents a paradox. On the one hand, visualizations are intended to help users learn about parts of their data that they don't know about. On the other hand, the more we know about the users' needs and the context of their data, the better we can design a visualization to serve them. The process described in this book embraces this paradox: it leverages the knowledge users have of their datasets, the context the data lives in, and the ways it was collected—including its likely flaws, challenges, and errors—in order to figure out the aspects of it that matter.

Put another way, this book is about the path from "I have some data…" to "We know this because of these clear, concise, and insightful visualizations." We believe that creating effective visualizations is itself a process of exploration and discovery. A good visualization design requires a deep understanding of the problem, data, and users.

Getting to Insight

We most often work with other people that have a dataset they are trying to make sense of. The process of designing a visualization usually starts when people walk into our office.

> CLIENT: I have some data that I'd like to visualize. How should I draw it?

The client seems to expect us to pull a visualization off the shelf, to sculpt that perfect visualization. We almost always frustrate them by asking what they hope to see.

> Q: What is it about the data that you would like to visualize?
>
> CLIENT: I want to see how profitable our stores are.
>
> Q: What in your data indicates a store being profitable?
>
> CLIENT: It means that the store has lots of sales of high-profit items.
>
> Q: How does profit vary by store?

And so on.

By the end of this process, we often find that the clients do not have a visualization problem, but an operationalization one. Their struggles to choose a visualization stem from a lack of clarity about which attributes of the data are most important and how those attributes relate to one another. Once they can describe how the data attributes relate to the question they are trying to answer, finding an appropriate visualization becomes much easier.

We have learned over the years that designing effective visualizations to make sense of data is not an art—it is a systematic and repeatable process. We have systematized this process into what we believe are reproducible and clear steps.

This process tracks our understanding of four components:

Data
> What data is available, and what does it mean? What does the data look like, and what are its important aspects? Where did it come from, and why was it originally collected?

Tasks
> What needs to happen with the data? What are the low-level questions and tasks that will support high-level goals?

Stakeholders
> Who is involved with the data, the problem, and the goals? What can they say about the problem to help design an effective visualization? Who will view the final visualization, and what sorts of things do we expect them to learn from it? What domain knowledge do they bring to the table? What answers would they find satisfying?

Visualization
> How does the understanding of data, tasks, and stakeholders come together? What representations of this data will fulfill the tasks for the users?

Regardless of the visualization outcome, this process will almost certainly lead to new discoveries and insights. These discoveries help to inform the operationalization, but they will also likely steer the process down new and unexpected paths. The guidance and framework in this book are meant to help identify opportunities for discovering new knowledge and to make an otherwise messy process a bit more structured.

Hotmap: Making Decisions with Data

As an example of how visualizations can help you to better understand a problem, and help an organization make decisions, we can look back to 2006. Microsoft was rolling out its new mapping tool,

Virtual Earth, a zoomable world map. The team behind Virtual Earth had lots of questions about how their users were using this new tool, so they collected usage data.

The usage data was based on traditional telemetry: it had great information on what cities were most viewed, how many viewers were in "street" mode versus "photograph" mode, and even information about viewers' displays. They instrumented search and navigation, and they collected counts for the number of times that users looked at certain sentinel regions. And because Virtual Earth was built on top of a set of progressively higher-resolution image tiles, the team was also archiving server logs that tracked how often individual tiles were downloaded.

Interviews with team members suggested that they did not have an intuitive notion of how their tool was being used. In conversation, one team member argued that people were likely to look at their own homes; another thought that the overhead photography would mostly be used over mountains. The goals were varied: they included seeing whether the user experience was well balanced across user needs and deciding how and where to invest in future rounds of photography.

We addressed these questions with a visualization tool called Hotmap. Figure 1-1 shows a screen capture from the visualization tool, focusing on the central United States. Hotmap uses a *heatmap* encoding of the tile access values. This is a visualization technique that uses a colormap to encode the access values at the geospatial locations of the tiles. Colored spots on the map are places where more users have accessed image tiles. The colormap is a logarithmic color scale, so bright spots have many more accesses than dim ones.

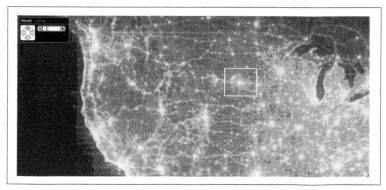

Figure 1-1. Hotmap, looking at the central United States. The white box surrounds an anomaly in South Dakota.

Some of the brightest areas correspond to major population centers —Chicago and Minneapolis on the right, Denver and Salt Lake City in the middle, and West Coast cities on the left. Near the center, though, is an anomalous shape: a bright spot where no big city exists. There is a star shape around the bright spot, and an arc of bright colors nearby. The spot is in a sparsely populated bit of South Dakota—there was no obvious reason to the team why users might zoom in there.

That point is, however, very close to the center of a map of the continental US. In fact, the team learned that the center of the star corresponds to the center of the default placement of the map in many browsers. The bright spot with the star most likely corresponds to users sliding around after inadvertently zooming in, trying to figure out where they've landed; the arc seems to correspond to variations in monitor proportions.

As a result of this usability challenge, many mapping tools—including Bing Maps (the successor product to Virtual Earth)—no longer offer a zoom slider, which keeps users from accidentally zooming all the way in on a single click.

A second screen capture, shown in Figure 1-2, reveals a bright spot off the coast of Ghana. This spot exhibits the same star pattern created by users scrolling around to try to figure out what part of the map they are viewing. This spot is likely only bright because it is at 0 degrees latitude, 0 degrees longitude, a point that GIS tools run into often. While computers might find (0,0) appealing, it is unlikely that there is much there for the typical Virtual Earth user to find interesting.[1]

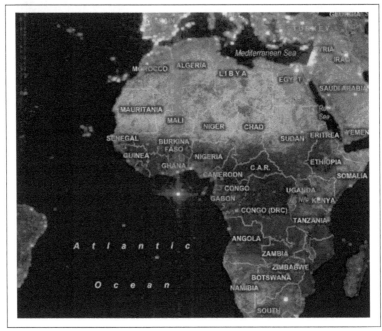

Figure 1-2. Hotmap, looking at the map origin (0,0).

This second bright spot inspired a hunt for bugs. The team rapidly learned that Virtual Earth's search facility would sometimes fail, and instead of returning an error message, typos and erroneous searches would sometimes redirect the user to (0,0). Interestingly, the bug had been on the backlog for some time because the team had decided that it was not likely to surface often. Seeing this image made it clear that some users really *were* being confused by the error, so the team prioritized the bug.

Although the Virtual Earth team started out using the Hotmap visualization expecting to find out about how users interacted with maps, they gleaned much more than just a characterization of usage patterns. Like many—dare we say most?—new visualizations, the

---

1 So many datasets have references to (0,0) that GIS practitioners refer to that location as "null island."

most interesting insights were those that the viewers were not anticipating to find.[2]

Where Visualization Is Useful

Is visualization the silver bullet to help us make sense of data? Not always. There are two questions to consider to help you decide if your data analysis problem is a good candidate for a visualization solution.

First, *could the analysis tasks be supported with an algorithm*? A crisp task such as "I want to know the total number of users who looked at Seattle" suggests that an algorithm, statistical test, or even a table of numbers might be the best way to answer the question. On the other hand, "How do users explore the map?" is much fuzzier. Fuzzy tasks are great candidates for a visualization solution because they require you to look at the data from different angles and perspectives, and to be able to make decisions and inferences based on your own knowledge and understanding.

The second question to consider is "Is all the necessary information contained in the dataset?" If there is information about the problem that is not in the dataset which requires an expert to interpret the data that is there, then visualization is a great solution. Going back to our fuzzy question about exploring a map, we can imagine that it is unlikely that there will be an explicit attribute in the data that classifies a user's exploration style. Instead, answering this question requires someone to interpret other aspects of the data to bring knowledge to bear about what aspects of the data imply an exploration style. Again, visualization enables this sort of flexible and user-centric analysis.

For all but the crispest questions about explicitly measured phenomena, visualization is probably a good tool to throw at a problem. In our experience, we have almost never come up against a problem that cannot benefit from some amount of visualization.

---

2 See "Further Reading" on page 8 for other stories of how Hotmap has been used.

Further Reading

The Hotmap project is discussed in:

- Fisher, Danyel. "Hotmap: Looking at Geographic Attention (*http://ieeexplore.ieee.org/document/4376139/*)." IEEE Transactions on Visualization and Computer Graphics 13 (2007): 1184–1191.
- Fisher, Danyel. "The Impact of Hotmap (*https://www.microsoft.com/en-us/research/publication/the-impact-of-hotmap/*)." The Infovis 2009 Discovery Exhibition. Redmond, WA: Microsoft, 2009.

CHAPTER 2

From Questions to Tasks

All visualization begins with a question about data. An analyst wants to know something about a phenomenon in the world, or wants to share their knowledge about it with someone else. She believes the phenomenon they wish to examine is represented somehow in the data.

The challenge in this process is that the question the analyst wishes to address can seem far from the data. The analyst might be working on a broad goal: say, "Are high-salary employees more productive than less well-paid ones?" This leads to a process of making the question measurable. What does the analyst mean by *high-salary*, and *productive*? What visualization or set of visualizations would demonstrate the relationship between these variables?

The process of breaking down these questions into something that can actually be computed from the data is iterative, exploratory, and sometimes surprising. This chapter describes how to refine high-level questions into specific, data-driven tasks. The outcome of that process is a set of concise design requirements for a visualization tool that supports finding answers to those questions.

The general concept of refining questions into tasks appears across all of the sciences. In many fields, the process is called *operationalization*, and refers to the process of reducing a complex set of factors to a single metric. The field of visualization takes on that goal more broadly: rather than attempting to identify a single metric, the analyst instead tries to look more holistically across the data to get a usable, actionable answer. Arriving at that answer might involve exploring multiple attributes, and using a number of views that allow the ideas to come together. Thus, operationalization in the context of visualization is the process of identifying tasks to be performed over the dataset that are a reasonable approximation of the high-level question of interest.

A visualization is not the inevitable outcome of operationalization. Exploring the data might show that the goal is best achieved with a statistical analysis or with machine learning. Similarly, the outcome of the process might show that a cluster analysis across multiple attributes is more useful than a plot. We find that more often than not, visualization is a vital component of getting to a successful operationalization.

This chapter emphasizes the data aspects of this process. The next chapter moves to the human side of the process: how to get the information necessary to effectively operationalize the high-level questions. Later chapters then look at how to translate the operationalized questions into specific visualizations.

Example: Identifying Good Movie Directors

To guide the process through operationalization, this chapter examines an exemplar question: "Who are the best movie directors?"

Nonspecific questions like this are how many data explorations start. Answering a question like this requires a much more specific task that can be precisely addressed with a dataset. Before we can be more specific, we first need to take a step back: who needs to know the answer to this question? The use case might be a film student trying to assert that his dissertation is about one of the most influential directors, or a hiring manager looking to hire a director for an upcoming project, or a journalist putting together a splashy article that will feature a top list.

Each of these users needs suggests different interpretations for the notion of *best* director. The film student is looking for a way to quantify and defend a notion of influence, whereas the hiring manager might want to limit themself to people working today who are less accomplished and thus more affordable. For this example, though, the user will be a journalist who is putting together an article about a new movie and wants to include a list of the best directors.

The goal of operationalization is to refine and clarify the question until the analyst can forge an explicit link between the data that they *can* find and the questions they *would like* to answer. For this example, the dataset at hand contains a list of movies rated by the film-aficionado community. Each movie is associated with a director, a number of raters, and an average rating score.

A Note on the Data

The dataset used for this chapter is comprised of two of IMDB's downloadable lists, *directors.list* and *ratings.list*. There is a copy of the Jupyter notebook (*http://jupyter.org/*) that parses them into cleaner CSVs on the book's companion website (*https://resour ces.oreilly.com/examples/0636920041320*). The script cleans the data to remove entries that the database refers to as not being movies, such as video games and TV shows. The analysis and visualizations in this chapter are carried out in Python (*https://www.python.org/*) and recorded in a second Jupyter notebook available at the same site.

With both data and a high-level question in hand, the visualization work can begin. Data alone is not enough to dictate a set of design requirements for constructing a visualization. What is missing here is a translation of the high-level question "Who are the best movie directors?" into a set of concrete tasks over the data.

The choice of dataset and operationalization is fundamentally a *specific perspective* on a problem; they stand in for what the analyst wishes to understand. In this example, there are other ways to frame the inquiry and other types of data that could be collected. This is a large part of why visualization is so important for answering questions like these: it allows an analyst's experience and knowledge to layer directly on top of the data that is ultimately shown. The analyst's skills and experience allow them to make inferences about the more abstract questions they are really interested in.

Making a Question Concrete

The process of operationalization winds its way from a general goal or a broad question to specific tasks, and then to visualizations that support those specific tasks based on concrete data.

To achieve this, the analyst searches for *proxies*. Proxies are partial and imperfect representations of the abstract thing that the analyst is really interested in. For example, *high movie ratings* may be a reasonable proxy for *best* in our movie example. Selecting and interpreting proxies requires judgment and expertise to assess how well, and with what sorts of limitations, they represent the abstract concept.

In operationalization, there are two important types of proxies:

- A proxy *task* is a lower-level task that stands in for the original. The result of a proxy task reflects on the answer to the original question, but the proxy task itself is more closely related to the data; it can be accomplished with quantitative tools, such as a visualization or a statistical analysis.

- A proxy *value* is an attribute in the data that stands in for a more abstract concept. This can be an existing attribute, or it can be derived from the data.

Operationalizing a question often results in more questions, which require further articulation of proxies. One step in this process is to find places where a question is underspecified or does not directly reference the data on hand, in order to identify where proxies are necessary.

Collaboration with stakeholders crucially informs the process of operationalizing questions. It helps to learn what data is available and how the results will be used. Interviews help to identify the questions and goals of the stakeholders with respect to the data and to further understand what data is available or can be made available. Throughout the process, an analyst translates questions and goals into a description of the problem that is amenable to a data solution. Interview techniques and prototyping are discussed in more detail in Chapter 3.

In this book we advocate an approach of systematic operationalization in order to bolster explicit acknowledgment, validation, and support of the range of possible proxy decisions for a question. This systematic approach leaves open future possibilities and provides guidance for making downstream decisions. The start to this process is getting to understand the question and what is available in the data—and appreciating the gaps between them.

This chapter both describes and illustrates the operationalization process. It uses the movie director example to show how to refine a question into detailed, specific tasks. It discusses the four components that we use to describe an operationalized task.

A Concrete Movie Question

The example started with the high-level question "Who are the best directors?" The dataset is a list of directors and a list of movies. The first task is to operationalize *best director*. As a rough definition, a good director has directed many good movies. But *many good movies* is also ill-defined, and thus a proxy for *good movie* might in turn be based on its rating on IMDB.

These decisions replaced one bit of ambiguity with three more. How many of these *best* directors need to appear in the results? What counts as *good* IMDB ratings, and what are *many* of them? For that matter, a quick glance at the IMDB data reveals that there are short films, TV episodes, video games, and so on—so what counts as a *movie*?

It is possible to choose the measures arbitrarily: "More than five movies with IMDB ratings greater than 9.8," or "average movie rating higher than 8.2," or "no movies with a rating less than 5." While it is not uncommon to make these sorts of decisions based on rough knowledge of the data, or even based on choosing nice, round numbers, looking at the actual data is important. The top-rated items on IMDB might turn out to have very high ratings but only one review. Great directors might direct a few stinkers, so just looking at the average rating might turn out to be a poor choice. The only way to learn what the data says is to start digging into it.

Choosing a proxy allows the analyst to sanity-check their decisions; it can be valuable to do this iteratively at each step, checking both the quality of the data and of the proxy.

A quick glance at the first five data items in the dataset reveals non-mainstream movies (Table 2-1). The alphabetical first movie in the dataset is called *#1*, with a total of 12 raters; the second is the similarly obscure *#1 Serial Killer*. Since the scenario targets a general audience, it should probably focus on movies that most people are likely to know. A different scenario could suggest very different proxies.

Table 2-1. A quick glance at the first data items in the movie dataset (which is sorted alphabetically) reveals that there could be movies with positive ratings that have very few raters, implying an obscure (but decent) movie.

ID	Raters	Score	Title	Director
0	12	6.4	#1 (2005)	Breen, James (V)
1	35	6.0	#1 Serial Killer (2013)	Yung, Stanley (I)
2	5	5.8	#137 (2011)	Elliott, Frances
3	11	7.4	#140Characters: A Documentary About Twitter (2...	Beasley, Bryan (I)
4	23	6.7	#30 (2013)	Wilde, Timothy
...	...	...	...	...

The decision to stick with mainstream movies suggests a need for a proxy for *popularity*. One choice could be the number of ratings for each movie. By plotting the distribution of the number of ratings by movies (Figure 2-1), we see that the vast majority of movies in the dataset actually have very few ratings.

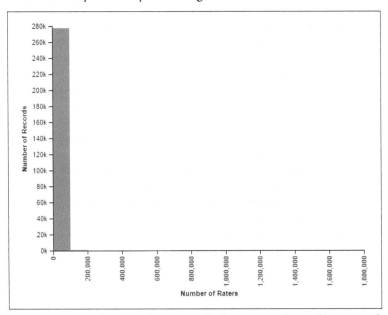

Figure 2-1. Distribution of ratings. This histogram shows the count of number of ratings per film. Almost all the films have few ratings, with a very long tail.

This first plot shows that the number of ratings is heavily skewed. One way to make this distribution more interpretable is to plot it on a logarithmic scale. In Figure 2-2, the data has been bucketed; a film with 1,000 ratings now appears in the bucket for $log_{10}(1000) = 3$. Taking the log of the number of ratings smooths the distribution, more effectively showing its shape.

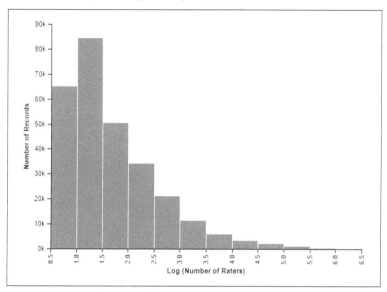

Figure 2-2. Distribution of the logarithm (base 10) of the number of ratings. The peak is under 2: most films have under 100 ratings.

We can also compute some basic summarizing statistics about the number of ratings: the median movie in the dataset has just 26 ratings while the 75th percentile is at 132 ratings.[1] By looking up the number of ratings for a sample of blockbusters, we note that movies that anyone can name offhand have tens of thousands of ratings. These are useful observations; perhaps it would be valuable to trim to a slimmer set of movies to ensure that most are ones that a reasonable number of people have seen.

We want to choose a number, though, that's fair to good movies, even if they are not very popular—in this case, we pick, somewhat

---

1 Median and percentile are ways of characterizing a distribution of numbers. If one were to sort the numbers, the 75th percentile would be 75% of the way down in the list. The median would be at the halfway point.

arbitrarily, the most-rated 25% of movies. This amounts to around 70,000 films with more than 132 ratings.

We next pivot and look at the distribution of ratings for the slimmed-down set of movies, shown in Figure 2-3. This distribution shows a distinct curve with a clear peak and noticeable drop-off: ratings above 7.5 seem different from lower ratings. (This distribution has a median score of 6.6, and a 75th percentile of 7.4.)

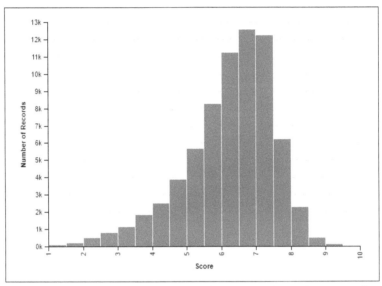

Figure 2-3. Distribution of score. This histogram shows the count of ratings, by bucket. Almost all ratings are extremely low, with a very gradual tail.

Stepping back from our dive into the data, we can observe that we have proceeded some distance along the operationalization. We have defined a good director and decided that it is based on their movies; we have focused on movies and chosen a set that are popular enough to be part of the analysis. But there are still unanswered questions: How will we rank directors against each other? What makes for a "best" director?

A systematic approach to operationalization allows an analyst to see the full range of decisions and helps in pulling together the set of proxies that can inform a final answer. Ultimately, an interactive visualization tool can enable exploration of multiple proxies to allow for a set of justified, and validated, answers. For our running example, we will continue with the operationalization after describing a framework for making decisions explicit throughout the process.

Breaking Down a Task

Throughout the operationalization, we need to identify *where* in a question or task there is a need for a more refined proxy. Doing so systematically can make it easier to validate those decisions, as well as to produce a road map of the process. This allows the analyst to effectively revisit decisions once a better understanding of the problem is gained.

An analyst can refine a task by first breaking it down into four specific components. Identifying these components and how they do or do not directly reference the data becomes a template for choosing more specific tasks. The components are:

Objects
> Things or events that exist in the world: in our example, a *director* and *a movie* are both objects. In other contexts, objects might be *a user* or *a sale of a single item*. When a task is specific enough, each object will be something that can be represented in or computed from, the data. Fairly often, when the task is at its most specific, an object will correspond to a single row in a database.

Measures
> The outcome variables that will be measured for the objects. *Quality of a director, happiness of a user*, and *sales of a store* are all measures. In a sufficiently specific task, the measure is either an existing attribute in the dataset or one that can be directly computed from the data. A measure is sometimes aggregated across many items of data. In our example, a number of movies are aggregated together to get a score for a single director.

Groupings (or partitions)
> Attributes or characteristics of the data that separate the data items into groups. For example, groupings might include *store region (western versus eastern), start date of players, whether users have purchased an upgrade*, or *sales by year*. In a specific task, partitions are attributes of the objects or can be calculated directly from those attributes. When the visualization is created,

partitions will often manifest as groupings, separations across charts, or filters.

Actions

Words that articulate the specific thing being done with the data, such as *compare, identify, characterize,* etc. Actions guide the process of choosing appropriate visualizations.

The action is useful for identifying the other components. Take this task: *Compare the amount of money spent in-game by players who play more hours versus those who play fewer hours.* The action is *compare.* What is compared? The *players* (the object). What is it about players that we want to compare? The *money spent* (the measure). Finally, there is a specific partition on the objects. They will be broken into two groups: those that play many hours and those that play few hours.

The following components are the heart of an iterative process:

1. Refine the question into one or more *tasks* that, individually or together, address the general question.

2. For each task:

    a. Identify the components of the task.

    b. Look for ambiguous components—namely, components that are not directly addressable by the dataset.

    c. For each ambiguous component, define a proxy by creating a new question that addresses the component, and return to step 1 with those questions.

    d. If there are no ambiguous components then the task is deemed actionable, and thus can be addressed with a visualization or other computational technique.

Next, we'll explicate some of the questions from the movie example to illustrate how the components work in practice, beginning with Example 2-1.

Example 2-1. Breaking down the task to find good directors

Task: Identify the top directors who have directed many good, popular movies

Action: Identify

Object: Director

Measure: Number of good, popular movies

Grouping: Filter out non-movies

Identifying top directors implies that there's a meaningful sort on the directors so that the top can be found (Example 2-2). Thus, we can further refine the action to specify an ordering. Also, our first look at the data showed that many movies are unpopular, which implied a grouping to filter out unpopular movies.

Example 2-2. Refined task for good directors

Task: Rank order of directors by those who have directed many good, popular movies

Action: Rank order

Object: Director

Measure: Number of good movies

Grouping: Filter out non-movies and unpopular movies

Filtering out unpopular movies is a subtask (Example 2-3), which we addressed with a histogram of the number of ratings for movies. The visualization of the distribution allowed us to determine a good cut point for popular versus unpopular—namely, popular movies were those in the top 25% of movies with the highest number of ratings.

> **Example 2-3. Subtask for filtering unpopular movies**
>
> **Task**: Filter out movies with significantly fewer ratings
>
> **Action**: Filter
>
> **Object**: Movie
>
> **Measure**: Number of ratings
>
> **Grouping**: Separate into most popular and least popular movies

This subtask can be brought back into Example 2-2 as a proxy for unpopular movies.

However, we still have some work to do on Example 2-2: the measure *number of good movies* is ill-defined with respect to the data. We need to refine this component by developing a proxy for a *good* movie. Once we do that, we can then examine what it means to have *directed many* of them.

These proxies require further elaboration. How *many* high-scoring movies are required from directors? Do low-scoring movies count against them? This process of identifying reasonable proxies is often iterative. For example, in exploring and validating a proxy with the data, it might become obvious that the effects of filtering by the number of ratings was a mistaken approach.

At this point, we can recognize that we need a proxy measure for *good* (Example 2-4). There are a variety of proxies that we can try here, with various visualizations. The process continues onward.

> **Example 2-4. Subtask for good movies**
>
> **Task**: Quantify "a good movie"
>
> **Action**: Quantify
>
> **Object**: Movie
>
> **Measure**: Goodness
>
> **Grouping**: None

Breaking down a task into components helps in guiding refinement of a task into one that can be addressed with the data. The most direct way to do so is to consider the question "Are the object, measure, and grouping each directly described in the data?" For each of these three components, is it clear which aspects of the data are important or how to derive what we need from the data? If not, repeat the process of formulating a subquestion in order to derive a more specific answer.

Let's take a look at a very different example—this time, from a gameplay metrics scenario (Example 2-5).

Example 2-5. Exemplar task for analyzing a game

Task: Compare the amount of money spent in-game by players who play more hours versus those who play fewer hours.

Action: Compare

Object: Players

Measure: Money spent

Grouping: Players who play many hours; players who play few hours

---

In Example 2-5, the partition divides between *many* and *few* hours. This component needs to be refined further, which leads to a new question: "In the game, how many is 'many' hours for a player?" The analyst might take a series of steps. They might look at the distribution of hours played, or they might choose to filter out players who have played zero hour or those who haven't made it past the tutorial, or they might look at other metrics that are important to the game. These steps would help the analyst figure out good proxies for *many* and *few* hours.

When Tasks Lead to New Questions

There are four broad categories of new lines of inquiry that can emerge from refining a question. First, as in the movie example, the refinement process often reveals that a new analysis is needed to answer these questions.

Second, operationalizing can also lead in new directions. In the process of exploring who the *best* directors are, the analyst might notice that some directors stick to a single genre; they might decide that this analysis might be interesting divided across multiple genres. They might also notice that both IMDB and Rotten Tomatoes have scores on movies, and want to see how these results vary based on Rotten Tomatoes scores instead of IMDB.

Third, the data itself can lead to new questions too. In exploratory data analysis (EDA), for example, the data analyst discovers new questions based on the data. The process of looking at the data to address some of these questions generates incidental visualizations —odd patterns, outliers, or surprising correlations that are worth looking into further.

Finally, doing some analysis often leads to doing a round of data cleaning. While data cleaning is largely out of the scope of this book, odd outliers and surprising trends are, as often as not, the result of dirty data.

Returning to the Example: Exploring Different Definitions

There are several different possible definitions of *best director*.

Here is one: the best director has the most movies with more than 134 ratings. Table 2-2 shows the top scorers. The most prolific directors in our dataset are Chuck Jones and Fritz Feleng (who directed classic Looney Tunes animations), William Hanna (who directed *Tom and Jerry* and other classic Hanna-Barbera cartoons), and George Méliès (an early inventor of special effects and shorts).

Table 2-2. Top five directors by number of films over threshold

Director	Avg. raters	Avg. score	Count	Total raters
Jones, Chuck (I)	719	7.4	148	106,397
Freleng, Fritz	402	7.2	141	56,730
Hanna, William (I)	591	7.5	119	70,315
Méliès, Georges	717	6.1	114	81,769
White, Jules (I)	235	7.1	102	23,969

Georges Méliès has 526 films on his IMDB page; only 114, however, made it over the threshold of raters. The huge number of films is explained by the fact that the films are shorts—more familiar on television now, but once also shown in theaters. This should be an opportunity to do more data cleaning to join in another table that will tell us whether a film is a short or not, and filter those out. IMDB has a film duration data table; in a typical analysis process, the next step would be to merge in this table, adding a new proxy for what makes for a *short* film.

We might explore other definitions of *best* directors. For example, the best directors might make the movies that people want to rate the most. Table 2-3 is a list of the directors whose movies have, in total, the most ratings.

Table 2-3. Top five directors by total number of ratings across all movies

Director	Avg. raters	Avg. score	Count	Total raters
Spielberg, Steven	245,717	7.2	36	8,845,795
Nolan, Christopher (I)	778,737	8.2	11	8,566,104
Tarantino, Quentin	526,689	7.8	13	6,846,955
Jackson, Peter (I)	371,219	7.6	16	5,939,505
Scorsese, Martin (I)	144,823	7.5	41	5,937,725

This list makes sense. These are very famous names who have directed very familiar movies.

Different proxies yield different results. Ordering by the average score for all movies by a single director might be one way to find the very best directors. As seen in Table 2-4, the first on this list is a director who has only one movie over the threshold: a Mongolian movie from 2016 with 624 raters and an average score of 9.7. This measure of popularity returns a very different set of results than the previous measure: ten thousand times more people rated Quentin Tarantino's movies than Uranchimeg Urtnasan's work.

Table 2-4. Top five directors by average score

Director	Avg. raters	Avg. score	Count	Total raters
Urtnasan, Uranchimeg	624	9.7	1	624
Miller, George (XXXVII)	394	9.6	2	787
Chowdhury, Amitabh Reza	14,628	96	1	14,628
Biebert, Aaron	12,040	9.6	1	1,204
Arsyn, Ken	619	9.5	6	3,712

But can the quality of a director be measured based on just one or two movies? Each step of data exploration leads to another step of refining the question. Is it more important to have many raters, a high average score, or a high minimum score?

The choice of metrics leads to very different outcomes. A slight tweak determines whether you find directors of animated cartoons, blockbuster directors, or a very diverse set of international directors.

How Specific Does the Process Get?

This process of refinement leads to a scary scenario. In Disney's *Fantasia*, in the Sorcerer's Apprentice sequence, Mickey Mouse attempts to stop an enchanted broom by chopping it in half and instead produces two half-size enchanted brooms. Will our analysis subtasks forever multiply?

The operationalization process is an iterative one and the end point is not precisely defined. The answer to the question of how far to go is, simply, far enough. The process is done when the task is directly actionable, using the data at hand. The analyst knows how to describe the objects, measures, and groupings in terms of the data— where to find it, how to compute, and how to aggregate it. At this point, they know what the question will look like and they know what they can do to get the answer.

An *actionable* task means that it is possible to act on its result. That action might be to present a useful result to a decision maker or to proceed to a next step in a different result. An answer is actionable when it no longer needs further work to make sense of it.

Low-level objects are ready to be interpreted from the data. Sometimes they can be read directly off the data table, but more often it is more indirect; the analyst may need to carry out transformations on the data, whether mathematical transformations or database joins. For instance, in the movie example, the object is the director; the proxy for the director is the result of aggregating multiple movies together. Partitions and measures at the lowest level will resolve to concrete manipulations of the objects.

The process ends when all the tools needed to answer a question are in place—whether as a number, a visualization, or even as an interaction across multiple visualizations representing multiple proxies. The analyst might decide that the right cutoff for *many hours* of gameplay is *six hours*—a number—or *the hours played by the top 10% of players*—a formula—or *above the logical breakpoint*, which might be represented by a distribution. These results get propagated back into any other tasks that depend on them.

Making Use of Results

This process of propagating results back into higher-level questions is flexibile. Sometimes the low-level question does not have an exact answer but instead resolves in its own visualization or interaction. That visualization might help an analyst in making a decision, but it might also imply parameters on the data. For example, the journalist might realize that there are several possible cutoffs for defining what it means to be a good movie. Rather than simply picking a specific threshold, an analyst might instead propagate a mechanism for dynamically determining cutoffs into higher-level tasks. Seeing a variable propagated like this can be a cue that an interactive visualization—rather than a static image—might be helpful.

Visualization is also important for supporting the operationalization process, even if the end result is not an interactive visualization. In the movie example, visualization helped us to understand the nature and distribution of the data. Visualization can be more prominent with more complex analysis tasks. If the analyst wanted to compare ratings against popularity, it would be difficult to display that on a list; if they wanted to explore hypotheses about how the popularity of directors changes over time, more visual representations would help them explore the data.

Conclusion: A Well-Operationalized Task

A well-operationalized task, relative to the underlying data, fulfills the following criteria:

- Can be computed based on the data
- Makes specific reference to the attributes of the data
- Has a traceable path from the high-level abstract questions to a set of concrete, actionable tasks

A well-operationalized task is a first step toward creating a visualization. Chapter 4 begins to describe the ways in which the objects, measures, and partitions can be shaped into aspects of a visualization. Chapters 5 and 6 construct visualizations based on them.

Written out in detail, this process can seem tedious, but in practice, it is abbreviated and simplified. There are two important uses for this systematization. First, the process of explicitly looking at components can help untangle knotty problems, decomposing places where the analyst has made assumptions about the data. Explaining precisely *why* the number of IMDB ratings is a proxy for popularity forces the analyst to explore whether it is a good choice—and, perhaps, to revise that choice later.

The process also helps guide questions and interviews. Chapter 3 explains how to carry out operationalization with domain experts. Recognizing the need to make decisions about proxies helps guide these conversations. Every dataset has subtleties; it can be far too easy to slip down rabbit holes of complications. Being systematic about the operationalization can help focus our conversations with experts, only introducing complications when needed.

Further Reading

The process outlined here is similar—and in many ways parallel—to the *Goal, Question, Metric* (GQM) process found in the software engineering space. GQM refines from a general goal to a specific metric, usually oriented around process improvement so that the consumer can have a single number that helps them know whether they are succeeding in improving that process.

Our process is more exploratory and often comes earlier in the cycle. A GQM analysis might choose a goal like "improve user retention." In contrast, exploratory operationalization might start with a question like "Do users come back to our site?" with the awareness that the problem is multifaceted and complex, and might require a variety of different metrics to describe. For more on GQM, see:

- Basili, Victor, Gianluigi Caldiera, and Dieter Rombach. "The Goal Question Metric Approach." Encyclopedia of Software Engineering. New York: Wiley, 1994.

The data visualization field has spent a great deal of effort trying to understand the tasks that can be accomplished in a visualization. Amar and Stasko, for example, explore a low-level analysis of tasks carried out on a specific visualization. At the other end of the spectrum, Brehmer and Munzner explore high-level tasks for visualization, starting with comparing presentation and exploration:

- Amar, Robert and John Stasko. "A Knowledge Task-Based Framework for the Design and Evaluation of Information Visualizations." Proceedings of the IEEE Symposium on Information Visualization (2004): 143–150.
- Brehmer, Mathew and Tamara Munzner. "A Multi-Level Typology of Abstract Visualization Tasks." *IEEE Transactions on Visualization and Computer Graphics* 19 (2013): 2376–2385.

CHAPTER 3

Data Counseling, Exploration, and Prototyping

The previous chapter outlined a way to analyze a real-world question and transform it into an actionable, operationalized task. This analysis involves many steps that require decisions along the way: identifying specific tasks that address the broad question; decomposing each task into specific objects, measures, and groupings; and finally building visualizations that validate and support these tasks. Carrying out this process effectively requires sophisticated domain expertise, knowledge of the data and the problem space, and a sense of what would be a good answer to the question. This chapter discusses a variety of techniques that support gaining this understanding through working with stakeholders and iterating on visualization prototypes.

We call this collaborative process *data counseling*. We chose this name because working with stakeholders is a back-and-forth process of conducting interviews; of diving deeply into a user's intents around data; and of understanding the stories of where the data comes from, what problems are associated with it, and what it can mean.[1] Data counseling is interwoven with exploring data, develop-

---

[1] This process is closely related to *task analysis* in interface design. The distinction is that task analysis is typically oriented towards creating interfaces; this process, instead, works with data, which warrants a unique set of considerations on the part of the designer.

ing visualization prototypes, and collecting feedback on these pre-liminary results. This chapter describes techniques for these steps as well.

A major visualization project can require multiple interviews and rounds of prototypes in an intensively collaborative process. Recognizing the ecosystem of stakeholders involved in a project can help uncover needs and increase the impact of the data analysis results. A smaller project might entail just one or two informal interviews and putting the data into a graphing program like Tableau.

Sometimes an analyst needs to make sense of data without a team around them. The strategies in this chapter still apply to prototyping and refining visualization solutions in such conditions. These techniques are applicable at all scales.

Technique 1: Data Counseling

Data counseling is a technique that brings domain expertise into the operationalization process to help inform decisions about good proxies as well as to uncover insights using the resulting visualizations. This expertise is uncovered through interviews with a variety of stakeholders in a project. The goal of these interviews is to gain an understanding of the questions and data, as well as to get feedback on proxies, explorations, and visualization designs.

Arguably, the hardest part of data counseling is figuring out *who* the stakeholders are and *what* questions to ask them. The rest of this section describes some of the types of stakeholders that can be encountered during this process and provides guidance for conducting interviews.

Identifying Stakeholders

When it comes to tackling a problem, who is invested in the results? Who will use the results, and who will they present those results to? If the visualization produces valuable insights who will act on those insights, and what will they do with them? There is likely a whole ecosystem of people that have been, are, or would like to be involved with the data and the problem—the people who produce and store the data, the people who want to consume it, and those who will make decisions based on it.

All the people who are invested in the problem in some way, shape, or form are the *stakeholders*. Identifying these stakeholders is crucial for data counseling. Different stakeholders can give different perspectives on the data and the problem, and potentially provide unanticipated paths to insight. The process of interviewing and examining the data itself may uncover new stakeholders who can provide fresh perspectives.

There are a number of recurring types of stakeholders. This list is by no means complete, but it can work as guidance for identifying some of the important people in the ecosystem of a problem. A single person could embody one, some, or all of these roles:

Analyst
> A person who works directly with the data, searching and exploring to make discoveries. These stakeholders are the people most likely to use visualizations designed for the problem.

Data producer
> A person who collects, creates, and curates the data. Data producers can often shed light on the nuances and quirks of how the data was attained and can be invaluable during the data cleaning process.

Gatekeeper
> A person with the power to approve or block the project, including authorizing people to spend time talking about the data and problem. The gatekeeper's perspective can be useful for understanding the high-level goals and potential impact of the project. In some settings, a gatekeeper may require a proposal to carry out an analysis.

Decision maker
> A person who wants to use the insights gleaned from the data to execute on a decision. Decision makers are often one step removed from analysts, and act as the analysts' customers. They often have a different interpretation of goals and questions than those who are closer to the data.

Connector
> A person who may not be directly involved with the data or the question but can identify other people to talk with. Connectors can help fit together diverse perspectives on a problem and fig-

ure out what analysis needs to happen. In our experience, good connectors are worth their weight in gold.

Conducting Interviews

The operationalization process proceeds through information gleaned from interviews; later rounds of interviews provide feedback on intermediate results and final designs. The role of the interviewer is to ask questions that will guide the stakeholders toward elucidating the information necessary for working through an operationalization and designing visualizations.

Interviewing can be very challenging, but it can also one of the best parts of the work—how many jobs allow you, even *require* you, to talk to experts about the deepest, most interesting parts of their problems? Interviewing is not easy, though, and requires practice and experience. The necessary skills include how to keep a conversation moving along and on track, how to elicit meaningful responses, how to revise questions based on responses, and how to interpret both subtle cues and detailed responses. While this section provides several strategies to help with these tasks, gaining competency in these skills is a matter of practice.

In conducting an interview, there is a sweet spot with regard to the amount of structure in the conversation. Unstructured interviews, on the one hand, resemble casual conversations—the interviewer goes in with little expectation of where the conversation will go and does little to guide it in any one direction. This style of interview can uncover unknown needs and goals, but it can take a significant amount of time to get to anything useful. On the other hand, formally structured interviews are like giving a stakeholder a verbal survey, where the interview is completely scripted and strictly guided. While efficient, this type of interview leaves little room for discovering new insights.

The most effective data counseling sessions aim for a spot in the middle: *semistructured interviews*. The interviewer does some preparation in developing initial questions. The rest of the interview is then open to exploring ideas that come up during the conversation. Be prepared, but also be open.

The initial set of questions for an interview should be open-ended and address the problem, data, and context in order to help understand where the interviewee sits: their perspective on the problem, how they see the scope of the problem, and how they expect to interact with it.

Some useful interview questions might include:

- What are the goals of the project? How do those goals fit with the organizational needs?

- Who would act on the insights and results of this analysis? What decisions are they looking to make?

- What questions can be answered with this data?

- What do you already know from the data, and what else do you expect to find?

- What do you want to do with the data that is not currently possible? If you could do that, what else would you want to do next?

These general questions are meant to get a conversation going and to help in establishing the start of the analysis process. They lead to more specific questions that help clarify understanding of the problem and the data, confront assumptions on the part of the stakeholder and the analyst, and shape the description of the problem into something that a visualization can solve.

Interviews often start in the wrong place

It is easy to begin this analysis in the wrong place. When people come to us with visualization questions, they often start with very specific questions: "How do I tie together two scatterplots with a gradient color pattern?" These types of questions tend to be the result of people struggling to force their data into the visualizations that they know best and finding that those either don't fully support the extent of the data they have or don't really support an insightful analysis.

The conversation searches out the more abstract question and often finds that the question the person really wants to solve has a very different visualization solution.

Librarians know this challenge well. When someone asks for, say, an issue of a news magazine, librarians are trained to gently probe for the underlying information need. What does the reader really want to know? Sometimes the question might be better solved with an entirely different source: if the reader who wants the latest *Time* magazine is hoping it will contain a map of Somalia, an atlas would fulfill their need better.

What would it look like in the data?

The process of data counseling often entails chasing down particular meanings of unclear words and identifying good proxies. The question "What would this look like in the data?" can lead to illuminating results. For example, if a journalist were trying to find "good movies" in the database, in the interview we might ask questions like "What would the data show for *good* movies?" and "What would *bad* movies look like?" This can help interviewees nail down specifics.

Fairly often, the interviewee will not be sure what a "good movie" would look like. The process of articulating a list of possibilities, as outlined in Chapter 2, can be highly informative in itself.

Making questions specific

Low-level questions arise when trying to make general tasks more concrete and actionable, such as defining what a specific dimension means or how the objects that appear in a task actually look in the data. Finding these poorly defined terms in the interview is a cue to ask more questions to clarify those concepts more concretely. It can be useful to ask stakeholders what these terms mean within their workflow or to show an aspect of the data by pulling it up in a spreadsheet.

Certain action terms are also useful cues during these interviews: the verbs a stakeholder uses when discussing data can help inform the visualization. For example, interviewees might talk about *comparing* data items in describing a task. This invites a follow-up question: "Would you like to compare one item to another, or group many items together?" Similarly, words such as *select, identify,* or *group* can translate directly into tasks that can be supported with a visualization.

Other words, like *shape, structure,* and *size,* can help in deciding what kinds of visual encodings to use or what characteristics of the data the stakeholder is most interested in seeing. The visualization types described in Chapters 5 and 6 will help you recognize and know what to do with visualization keywords like these during interviews.

Breaking out of dead ends

Interviews can reach a point that feels like a dead end: the stakeholder has answered the planned question but the problem still seems inscrutable. There are a couple of strategies that can be used here:

- Try to rephrase the stakeholder's response back to them. This strategy allows the stakeholder to correct any misinterpretations and it also can prompt the stakeholder to explain their ideas in a more familiar terms.

- Try to ask the same or similar questions in different ways. Often a specific phrase or choice of words will click with the stakeholder and cause them to respond in a way that makes more sense.

- Try exploring a different conversational topic. It's not unusual that another topic will illuminate this one.

One of the most important things you can do in interviews is to keep the stakeholders talking. The more they talk, the more likely it is that they will share a response that clarifies a topic or opens up a new avenue of inquiry.

The interviewer's toolbox

There are several tools that are a part of the interview toolkit. Commonly used interviewing tools include pen and paper, voice recorder, camera, and video recorder. We advocate for voice recording of interviews, in large part because it is difficult to take detailed notes while also trying to think of follow-up questions based on what is being said. We try to transcribe an interview shortly after it is conducted to ensure the context is fresh in our minds. We rarely transcribe an interview word for word, but instead transcribe the most important or complex details. Transcribing is useful for analyzing the interview results, as well as for making it easy to refer back to the conversation later in the design process.

Conducting Contextual Interviews

In general, a first interview does not get into detailed analysis; it can be useful to get a general overview of the problem, identify stakeholders, and establish the stakeholders' expertise. It is in follow-up interviews where details begin to emerge.

There is often a big difference between talking to someone in a conference room as opposed to sitting at their desk. In a conference room, people will often tell a very general story; at their desks, they will more likely show their processes in very specific ways. For follow-up interviews, the *contextual interview* is a particularly useful tool. Contextual interviews take place in the stakeholder's work environment and consist of demonstrations of the tools and data inspection methods that the stakeholder currently uses. These types of interviews can bring to light aspects of a problem that might not have come up in a strictly verbal interview. They help show how the data works in practice: what happens with current capabilities and how users handle and understand the data they see.

A contextual interview often starts by asking the stakeholder to either walk through a specific analysis task they have already performed or conduct some of their work for that day with the interviewer present. The stakeholder talks through each step they are taking; the interviewer can interrupt with clarifying questions or use these as launching points for further explorations. The following starting questions can help the interviewer understand what works, what does not work, and what does not yet exist:

- What is the work process you currently use? What tools are involved?
- What challenges do you have in analyzing the data?
- Are there limitations within the system? If so, how do you work around them?
- Do you understand what the system is doing to the data and any algorithms that are being applied, or is this a black box?

Technique 2: Exploring the Data

While talking with stakeholders can be very informative, there is no substitute for reaching deep into the data. We like to start exploring the data as early as possible, for a few reasons. First, it is useful to understand how it is structured and what data is available. Second, each operationalization needs to be checked against the data, and third, it helps to start addressing fine-grained tasks.

In Chapter 2, for example, exploring the data helped us determine which fields were available in trying to evaluate what would make for a good director. It also helped us choose appropriate cutoffs in trying to define terms like *highly rated movie.*

Working through the analysis, then, brings forward a variety of visualization tools to explore the data. Tools like Excel and Tableau, or R and Pandas (*http://pandas.pydata.org/*), make it easy to rapidly generate visualizations that can highlight distributions of data, its major dimensions, and the values within. These tools also make it easy to check whether a dataset makes sense—for example, to confirm that a hierarchy really is layered appropriately or to ensure that there are only a small number of categories for a specific dimension of the data.

Sometimes it becomes clear that the problem is so specialized that it needs a bespoke visualization tool created from scratch. This happens when the data to be explored is not amenable to an off-the-shelf tool. Both Hotmap, described in the Preface, and the case study in Chapter 8 are examples of situations in which it was necessary to explore complex data with novel visuals. These bespoke tools can be created using visualization-specific languages like Vega (*https:// vega.github.io/vega/*), D3 (*https://d3js.org/*), or Processing (*https:// processing.org/*).

These can be fast-and-loose data prototypes: the goal is to get ideas up and going as quickly as possible, as opposed to carefully considering software architecture for long-term use and reusability. Rapidly discarding bad prototypes is as much a critical part of visualization as it is of other design areas.

Making the decision to create a custom data exploration tool requires weighing the development time against the significance of the analysis—if it is possible to get 80% of the way to a good decision using Excel, then it may not be worth spending three months to develop a custom solution. Bespoke exploration visualization tools instead come into play later, when an operationalization is well established and verified, and the focus is on going back and answering the high-level question.

If the high-level goals of a project can often be met with off-the-shelf tools then it is great to be considered a hero for quickly resolving the problem! Custom tools, in contrast, can be great ways to better understand what is lacking in the current ecosystem of visualizations. These insights are invaluable when designing a custom visualization tool.

One challenge is knowing when, and how, to start digging into the data. Oftentimes the stakeholders already have some way of analyzing or visualizing the data that they find to be insufficient for their question. This is usually good place to start. For example, are they looking at many static visualizations? Add interactivity to support exploration. Are they using only one kind of visualization? Take a different perspective on the data and visualize it in a different way using another type of visualization. Use these early data explorations for a deeper conversation about what works and what doesn't, and why. This process also provides a chance to better understand the stakeholders' perspectives on the data. Chapter 8 discusses a case study where scientists had a pre-existing set of technologies; adding interactivity and new representations helped reveal that there were entirely new questions to ask, too.

Technique 3: Rapid Prototyping for Design

Even from fairly early stages in the process, prototypes of the final tool can be a helpful model. The intention behind prototypes is to explore the visualization *design space*, as opposed to the *data space*. A typical project usually entails a series of prototypes; each is a tool to gather feedback from stakeholders and help explore different ways to most effectively support the higher-level questions that they have. The repeated feedback also helps validate the operationalization along the way.

Rapid prototyping is a process of trying out many visualization ideas as quickly as possible and getting feedback from stakeholders on their efficacy. Throughout the data counseling process, multiple rounds of rapid prototyping can help in understanding how the problem is formulated. In early phases, sketches on a whiteboard can help to better understand what types of visualizations to use and how stakeholders might interact with them. Later on, higher-fidelity techniques can explore the space of possible visualization designs. The design concept of "failing fast" informs this: by exploring many different possible visual representations, it quickly becomes clear which tasks are supported by which techniques.

The Range of Prototypes

The term *prototypes* refers to a broad range of techniques and tools, from paper to programming. The fidelity of these prototypes, as well as the time and energy required to create them, lives on a spectrum (Figure 3-1).

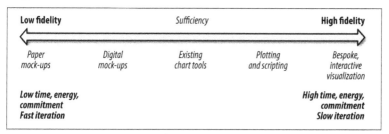

Figure 3-1. Prototypes range from low-fidelity sketches to high-fidelity working models.

One end of the spectrum is characterized by *low-fidelity* (or *lo-fi*) prototypes. These include mock-ups quickly sketched on paper or a whiteboard with impressions of what the data might look like, and fast, digital mock-ups that may include some controls for explaining interaction ideas, such as slide jumps in PowerPoint or Keynote. Figure 3-2 is an example of a quick interface mock-up made during the design process. Lo-fi digital mock-ups can also incorporate charts generated in a tool like Excel or Tableau with fake or sampled data to explore possible visualization representation ideas. These lo-fi prototypes are great for communicating the gist of an idea in an interview, or for recording high-level ideas when planning out how to explore the data. Lo-fi prototypes are, by nature, fast and easy to produce.

Lo-fi sketches play a critical role in interviews. Creating these prototypes can help us to understand what the implications of the data might be, and clarify the usefulness of different proxies. If a diagram is confusing to explain and design on a whiteboard, it may require too much detail to fit on a screen.

Communicating ideas with lo-fi prototypes can rapidly help establish whether the visualization designer is on the same page as the stakeholders. Drawing pictures of possible interfaces can start new conversations about the problem and its constraints. Figure 3-2 shows one instance: a stakeholder was discussing relational data, and drawing this data on the whiteboard allowed the stakeholder to see what it might feel like to visualize the data as a network. The multiple colored lines allowed the stakeholder to start thinking about how to view multiple modalities of the data; the directed edges were actually built from a sample of the data. Drawing this prototype helped the client realize that there was more structure to the data then they had been communicating: every node in the graph represented by a box actually occurred at a specific time, and it was important in the analysis to expose the temporal dimension of the data.

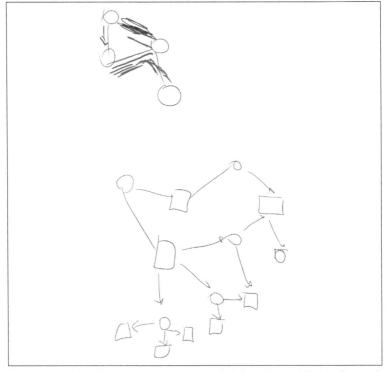

Figure 3-2. A lo-fi prototype exploring the idea of a weighted, directed graph layout. This sketch was hand-drawn on a whiteboard during an interview session, based on sample data, by manually looking at the spreadsheet and drawing out the relationships.

Lo-fi *slideware* can help ensure that designs will make sense to users, especially when incorporating interactive features into the design. The slideware in Figure 3-3 shows one step in the feedback cycle, illustrating the result of a specific interaction mechanism. This image was manually assembled in a variety of different tools. The prototype sketch is meant to help the user understand how the final interaction will work.

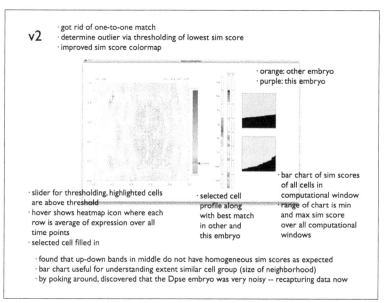

Figure 3-3. This slideware image of a design stage shows iteration from a previous version. The images were created in a variety of different tools.

On the other end of the prototype spectrum are *high-fidelity* (or *hi-fi*) custom visualizations which must be created from scratch. These hi-fi prototypes are meant to largely contain the core functionality of an envisioned visualization tool, including all necessary visualizations of the data and interaction mechanisms. They will often, however, gloss over many backend issues such as smooth integration with existing workflows or fully fleshed out features for saving and loading. Just as for bespoke visualizations created for our own data exploration, languages like D3 or Processing can help in creating hi-fi prototypes rapidly.

Hi-fi prototypes are meant to be thrown away. In our experience, however, hi-fi prototypes are often the tools that get deployed and adopted by some users, particularly to those frantic to get into their data. Regardless, the point is not to worry about the code other than to confirm that ideas can work.

Using a Data Management Pipeline

Using a data analytics engine to handle data management can allow an analyst to rapidly iterate through different ways of looking at the data. Many off-the-shelf data visualization systems provide both a data pipeline, which consists of database connectors and data cleaning and shaping facilities, and a visualization system. Until recently, however, doing this prototyping meant that analysts were constrained to the visual mappings available in the system.

A few tools have begun to allow developers to incorporate their own custom visuals: Google Sheets, Microsoft Excel, and Microsoft PowerBI (*https://powerbi.microsoft.com/en-us/*) all have custom add-in mechanisms. PowerBI also provides dashboard tools like cross-filtering between custom add-ins.

Eliciting Feedback

Identifying stakeholders during data counseling is useful not only to help with the operationalization, but also to garner feedback on prototypes. With rapid prototyping as a strategy, we go back to our stakeholders early and often with our visualizations to ensure that the operationalization has directed an effective visualization.

Eliciting useful feedback, however, goes beyond asking stakeholders if they like what they see—approval is necessary, but not sufficient. Part of the problem with seeking approval is that interviewees (sometimes unconsciously) wish to give positive feedback to an interviewer; this can be particularly problematic within a friendly team. A stakeholder might say they like a visualization that is not informative but looks nice.

We like to focus instead on what the visualization can and cannot do. A contextual interview where the stakeholder uses the visualization can be particularly insightful for uncovering weaknesses in the design or problems with the operationalization. Keeping questions focused on aspects of the data that are being shown forces the stakeholder to more directly confirm or refute the efficacy of what they are seeing.

And, Repeat

It is very difficult to get a good (or even adequate) operationalization of a problem the first time around. Getting this right often requires multiple interviews with stakeholders, interspersed with some data exploration and rapid prototyping.

For example, consider an operationalization that leads to a distribution of values in a histogram. That distribution helps show that there are outliers at one end of the range that had not been in the original problem description; stakeholders may then realize the outliers are actually quite interesting, which leads to a new task and a new representation.

The process is often a very iterative one. Talk with some stakeholders, try some ideas with the data, share those ideas with the stakeholders. And, repeat.

Conclusion

This chapter looked at several core techniques for supporting operationalization: data counseling, data exploration, and rapid prototyping. These techniques bring a variety of different perspectives on the problem and the data in order to build, refine, and support an operationalization of a problem. All of these techniques are useful on their own, but using them in combination provides a powerful suite of tools.

Chapter 4 looks at the nature of the data itself. Understanding the types of data, and the tasks that can be carried out with it, leads to Chapter 5 and a look at the core visualizations for basic data types.

Components of a Visualization

The previous two chapters outlined the process of refining a question into tasks. Chapter 2 broke each task down into components: *actions*, *objects*, *measures*, and *partitions*. These terms help identify where and how to turn fuzzy tasks into specific, actionable ones. Then, Chapter 3 discussed in more detail how to solicit the use scenarios and user stories that motivate the decisions made about proxies during operationalization.

The process in Chapter 2 concluded with a well-operationalized task and promised that this can lead to a visualization. But it did not discuss *how* to translate an operationalized task into a visualization. There is one step left before we can start doing visualization: we must understand the data..

This chapter takes the first step to translating these descriptions into visualizations. Understanding the characteristics of the data will make it easier to select an appropriate visualization. Chapter 5 then describes specific visualizations to match the data characteristics outlined here—more specifically, its dimensions and measures, how it is grouped and aggregated. In Chapter 6, we'll look at how views can be combined to support rich, dynamic analysis of complex tasks and data.

Dimensions and Measures

The attributes of the data serve particular roles in a task. A *dimension* is an attribute that groups, separates, or filters data items. A *measure* is an attribute that addresses the question of interest and that the analyst expects to vary across the dimensions. Both the measures and the dimensions might be attributes directly found in the dataset or derived attributes calculated from the existing data.

In different fields, these terms get somewhat different names. In the sciences, it's more common to talk about *independent variables* (those that the experimenter manipulates) and *dependent variables* (the outcomes of the experiment). The intuition is the same for task operationalization, although in many business intelligence scenarios, for example, the data analyst cannot actually control who walks into the store or visits the website.

The term *metric* is sometimes used to describe a measure that stands as a proxy for a desired value.[1] One virtue of a visualization approach is the ability to handle multiple metrics at once. Rather than trying to reduce everything to a single number, the analyst can look at several different measures. For example, it is reasonable to say "The fastest route is getting faster, and that's good, but the variance is really brutal." Chapter 6 discusses several techniques to visualize multiple metrics.

Example: International Towing & Ice Cream

This section discusses different data types with a motivating example. Sue is a data analyst for International Towing & Ice Cream (ITIC), a fictional company that provides a variety of important roadside services. ITIC's products and services are purchased on the road, so their location is important—and, as in any ice cream delivery service, so is the temperature (Table 4-1).

---

1 Though the distinction between a *metric* and a *measure* makes for entertaining online debates, this book sees the two as effectively synonymous.

Table 4-1. Sample metrics

Time	Customer	Sales location (lat)	Sales location (lon)	Product category	Product	Temperature	Revenue
June 17, 10:30 am	0121	47.6062	-122.332	Roadside	Towing	84	$100
June 17, 10:35 am	0232	33.26	-112.04	Roadside	Flat	96	$50
June 17, 10:37 am	0304	37.52	-122.16	Delivery	Ice cream	103	$10

The operationalization and data counseling process helped Sue realize that she wants to display sales grouped by product categories. Because product purchases vary over time—on a daily cycle, a weekly rhythm, and by season—she will want to look at sales, divided among categories, over time and locations. For example, Sue might look at the total revenue by product; in this case, the product is the dimension, while the revenue is a measure.

Dimensions

The *dimensions* of the data are the ways in which the data varies. Chapter 2 discussed partitions on the data; these partitions can be seen as dimensions.

In the ITIC example, there are a number of dimensions:

- Temperature
- Time
- Product
- Location

There are several different *types* of data here. When choosing good visualizations to explore data, it is important to recognize the type, as different charts are designed to optimize different data types. For example, a visualization that works well for showing time of day may not be effective for showing geospatial location.

The next section looks at the types of data used in visualizations; the visualizations in Chapter 5 are indexed on these data types. A user may have data that needs to be changed into a different representation. The following section describes a selection of ways to transform between data types.

Types of Data

Chapter 5 examines a variety of charts. The charts are indexed to the user task and can be selected based on the types of dimensions and measures.

Data attributes can be divided into three principal types:

Continuous (interval and ratio) data
Consists of ordered, equally and meaningfully spaced values. Ratio data has a meaningful zero point, and so can be added or subtracted: 10 feet plus 20 feet adds to 30 feet. Interval values, on the other hand, lack a meaningful zero point. As such, differences between interval values can be computed, but two interval values cannot be added together: values like dates, pH readings, and oven temperatures are interval data. In the ITIC example, the temperature and time of day are both continuous data. In many scenarios, ratio data is a likely measure: revenue and sales amount are examples of ratio data.

Ordinal data
Consists of discrete values that are ordered, but that cannot be meaningfully added or subtracted. Rankings are a good example of ordinal data: if a runner comes in first in one race and ninth in another, they did not come in a total of tenth, and it is not clear how to compare them to the runner who came in fifth twice.

Categorical data
Consists of discrete values; every item falls into a single category. Categorical data has no particular ordering—*north* does not logically come before or after *west*. In visualization, knowing something about the cardinality—the number of distinct values—of categorical data is important. In using categorical data for an axis or a color scale, there should be few enough categories that it makes sense to group the data into them and for the list of categories to be readable and comparable.

In addition, there are three specialized forms of data that are worth discussing on their own as they have specific mappings to visualization chart types:

Temporal data

> This is a form of interval data that has a time component. While a single timestamp refers to a single time (e.g., "November 20, 2010, 8:01 am"), it can be interpreted in a broad variety of ways.

> Temporal data is often interpreted cyclically and hierarchically. Time comes in cycles (e.g., "every day at 8:00 am," or "weekdays from 8 to 9 am"). Time may be grouped into ranges (e.g., "November 2010"), and can be placed against a number of calendars (e.g., fiscal years, calendar years, workdays). Times can be subtracted to get a *duration*, which is ratio data. Visualization toolkits often offer powerful tools for organizing temporal data.

Geographical data

> Refers to places; it is inherently two-dimensional (or three-dimensional, in some cases). It may come in the form of positions, outlines of shapes, or names of places. It can often be grouped into categorical data with the help of an atlas to assign zip codes, city names, or other relevant groupings.

Relational data

> This is data that connects two other points: this might be from a *hierarchy* or a *network*. For example, the fact that some number of commuters go from one place to another is relational data; so is the fact that one person reports to another. When data items are categorized, they sometimes are represented as relational; the relation is between the data item and its category.

Transforming Between Dimension Types

Different data types can be difficult to fit into particular visualization types. Often, transforming between data types may help simplify the data into a form that can be processed more easily. This section highlights a few of the most common and useful transformations:

Categorical-to-ordinal and ordinal-to-categorical

> Categorical data almost always has to be interpreted in some order or another. Conversely, many visualizations are marked as taking categorical data when the user has ordinal data. Each type may be interpreted as the other, as needed, ensuring that the order in ordinal data is always preserved.

Continuous to ordinal

Continuous data can be difficult to deal with as a dimension so it is sometimes transformed into ordinal data. In the ITIC example, the analyst might group a number of entries together into *hot* and *cool* temperatures, or might separate *mornings* and *afternoons*. This process makes analysis far more tractable—it is useful to make statements like "We sold twice as much ice cream on hot days as we did on cool days." Unfortunately, this imposes a hard line on otherwise smooth data: if 80 degrees and above is considered hot, then a day when it's one degree cooler (-79 degrees) is now a qualitatively different sort of day than an 80-degree day. When a continuous measure is broken into ordered groups, it is referred to as *binning*.

Ordinal to continuous

While ordinal values cannot be directly added, they can be assigned point values. This is familiar from sporting events, like the Olympics, where top scores tend to be very similar. As such, the rank is a more useful measure then the actual value. To assign overall winners across multiple rounds, though, each rank is transformed into points. The points can then be added and ranked.

Reducing cardinality for categorical data

Categorical data refers to the data column within its context. A company's entire product catalog probably has too many items to be analyzed with categorical techniques unless the analyst is looking specifically at a particular subproduct. Rolling together smaller categories into an *other* category, for example, can reduce cardinality; so can finding implicit or explicit hierarchies in the data.

Drilldowns

The drilldown is a common interactive technique between several hierarchical dimensions. *Drilling down* merely means moving the focus of attention from a higher-level dimension to a single, lower-level component: an analyst might drill down from a view that shows multiple years to focus on the year 2012, and then look at the months within it. Drilling from nation to region to state to city is common, or from business units to teams, or feature areas in telemetry data to features to specific events.

Rollups

The rollup is the logical opposite of the drilldown: grouping items that share a hierarchical level and shifting the focus up a level.

Pivoting data

The pivot operation summarizes items that have been grouped together. For example, in the ITIC example, communicating total revenue by product category would require that the data be pivoted along that column. (Roadside total revenue would then add to $150; total delivery to $10.)

Pivoting in Tools

Pivoting can be initially confusing to many data analysts, despite its tremendous power. Microsoft Excel does not pivot data by default: given a table of numbers, Excel plots the first column on the x-axis and the second on the y-axis. This can be difficult to work with if you have raw data. Tools like Excel's Pivot Tables, Tableau, and Microsoft PowerBI all work instead on pivoted data. In R, the pivot operation is supported with the plyr package; conveniently, Pandas calls the operation "pivot."

Dimensionality Reduction and Clustering

In the machine learning work that is increasingly important for dealing with large datasets, some core techniques fall under the umbrellas of dimensionality reduction and clustering. Although it is far outside the scope of this book to discuss how these techniques work, it is worth briefly considering what these techniques do to data for consideration in an operationalization.

Dimensionality reduction is a way of reducing a large number of different measures into a smaller set of metrics. The intent is that the reduced metrics are a simpler description of the complex space that retains most of the meaning. For example, a movie recommendation service might keep hundreds of individual dimensions about a user, such as the set of movies that she has reviewed and watched. These dimensions are both difficult to interpret alone and far too sparse to be useful: most movies have been watched by comparatively few users. Dimensionality reduction attempts to reduce these to a smaller set of useful dimensions, such as "likes horror movies," which can be more directly analyzed and inspected. The outcome dimensions are usually continuous; depending on the technique, they may even produce ratio data, so that one movie is *twice* as much a horror film as another.

Clustering techniques are similarly useful for reducing a large number of items into a smaller set of groups. A *clustering* technique finds groups of items that are logically near each other and gathers them together. For example, the movie recommender service might cluster users into groups. Analysts can then carry out analyses on individual groups.

Examining Actions

Chapter 2 discussed some of the core *actions* in tasks, but left the concept rather broad. The action helps identify candidate visualizations and encodings. Some single visualizations can address multiple actions: a bar chart can allow a user to find a specific value, identify the largest or smallest value, roughly guess an average, or compare two or more bars to each other. On the other hand, some tasks are particularly well-supported by one visualization or another; for example, a node-link diagram can be great for tracing paths through a network.

Some of the actions that often come up describe:

- Finding and reading individual values in the data
- Characterizing the distribution of a dimension: minimum, maximum, outliers, central tendency, sort order, etc.
- Identifying the trend of a metric over time (or some other dimension)

There are also more complex actions:

- Comparing a value across a category ("dollars from store A versus store B")
- Comparing a metric to another metric ("height versus weight of subjects" or "salary distribution of men versus women")
- Contrasting a metric with many others ("Seattle versus other cities")
- Clustering values ("divide consumers into market segments")

Many of these actions look like statistical tasks (e.g., "I want to know if men or women spend, on average, more money at our store"), Indeed, if an analyst needs only one or two of these tasks—"I want to know if men or women spend an average of more money at our store"—then a visualization probably is not necessary.

Multiple tasks, however, are often linked: an analyst may want to be able to explore the distribution to find reasonable cutoffs, or explore subdivisions of the data across a range of different dimensions. For example, an analyst may want to see how a distribution of product sales looks when the data is partitioned by store, or product, or even by the display aisle, or an analyst may want to switch from making comparisons of older women versus younger women to older women versus older men. A visualization tool can often support this more open-ended exploration better than statistical tests.

Action keywords can cue which visualization to use. Tasks like "Compare one object to another across multiple dimensions" are a cue that the analyst might want to compare multiple series. In contrast, "How is this item different?" suggests that the analyst might want to pull out a single item to compare to a background set of items. "Are any items different?" is a cue to look for visualizations that help show outliers.

The next two chapters look at how to choose a visualization based on the operationalization and the concepts described here.

Single Views

It does not necessarily take a sophisticated visual representation to make a compelling point or understand a complex dataset. Many of the most discussed, most viral, and most interesting visualizations are based on basic chart types. In this chapter, we'll take a look at some of the familiar core chart types. This is well-trodden territory —a sample of some different approaches can be found in "Further Reading" on page 83, including attempts to taxonomize the space in different ways.

This chapter takes a somewhat different approach to organizing core chart types. It is organized around the things that the analyst knows, and wants to know, about the data. This follows from the process of operationalizing the data (Chapter 2), interviewing users (Chapter 3), and understanding the data's shape and the actions we can take with it (Chapter 4). The operationalization has helped reveal something about *how the data is structured* and *what questions there are about it*. This knowledge can be used to select chart types based on specific data questions.

Depending on the analyst's task and question, visualizations can emphasize different results from the same dataset. For example, the United States Consumer Financial Protection Bureau (CFPB) has released information about consumer complaints and how they were resolved across a number of different financial products. Among other columns, the data describes the class of financial products to which a complaint applies and the type of relief that the complaint received. The examples in the following figures aggregate that data to just three dimensions: the product, the number of claims that had some form of relief, and the number of claims that did not.

Data Sources and Demos

The data sources used in this chapter were collected from publicly available repositories. The raw data is cited in "Datasets" on page 85 and on the book's website (*https://resources.oreilly.com/examples/ 0636920041320*). These examples are not meant to be used to draw broad conclusions; in many cases, the data is simplified for illustrative purposes.

Interactive Vega and VegaLite code to create most of the visualizations in this chapter and in Chapter 6 can also be found on the book's website.

Different chart types support different types of questions. If the analyst wants to see how two different groups compare relative to each other, a scatterplot (Figure 5-1) might be an appropriate choice. If the numbers are components of a larger value, they can be added together to get a stacked bar chart (Figure 5-2). Conversely, to compare the numbers to *each other*, the analyst might choose a clustered bar chart (Figures 5-3 and 5-4).

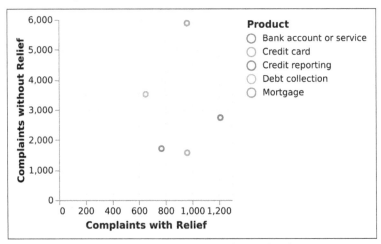

Figure 5-1. A scatterplot emphasizes the relationship between cases that received relief and those that did not for five different products.

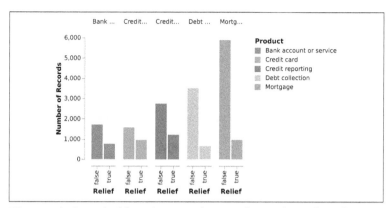

Figure 5-2. A stacked bar chart emphasizes the total number of complaints.

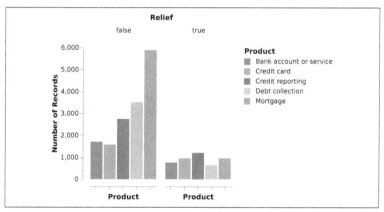

Figure 5-3. A clustered bar chart emphasizes the contrast between the number of people who requested relief and those who attained it.

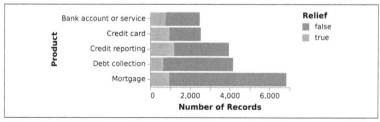

Figure 5-4. A different clustering emphasizes the different sizes of the populations who didn't receive relief (and the similarity of those who did).

The list of visuals in this section can never be exhaustive, and new chart types are being created all the time. This set, however, addresses many of the major categories and the vast majority of charts found in the wild. The list of charts is arranged by a set of common data questions according to which they are most effective at supporting.

This chapter first gives a quick primer of perceptual concepts that underlie the construction of these basic charts. After that, the charts are organized by data question. An overview of that organization is shown in Table 5-1. The language here is intentionally informal because it is meant to work as a reference for helping to map an operationalization to visualization solutions.

Table 5-1 uses the data types from "Types of Data" on page 48. *C* is for categorical, *Q* for continuous (quantitative), and *O* for ordinal data. *V* represents any data type that can be mapped to a drawing attribute, like color or line thickness. If a drawing supports $Q \times Q$, that means it supports a dataset with two continuous columns.

Table 5-1. Questions and their corresponding visualizations in this chapter

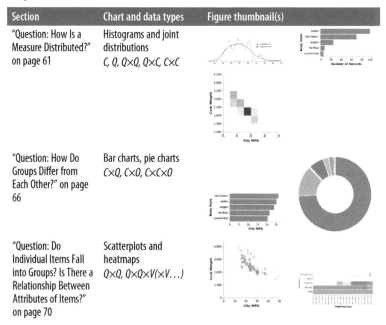

Section	Chart and data types	Figure thumbnail(s)
"Question: How Is a Measure Distributed?" on page 61	Histograms and joint distributions *C, Q, Q×Q, Q×C, C×C*	
"Question: How Do Groups Differ from Each Other?" on page 66	Bar charts, pie charts *C×Q, C×O, C×C×O*	
"Question: Do Individual Items Fall into Groups? Is There a Relationship Between Attributes of Items?" on page 70	Scatterplots and heatmaps *Q×Q, Q×Q×V(×V...)*	

Section	Chart and data types	Figure thumbnail(s)
"Question: How Does an Attribute Vary Continuously?" on page 72	Line charts $Q \times O$, $Q \times C \times O$	
"Question: How Are Objects Related to Each Other in a Network or Hierarchy?" on page 73	Network visualizations Network (×V...) on nodes and edges	
	Tree visualizations Network (×V...) on nodes and edges; Network×Q×V on nodes	
"Question: Where Are Objects Located?" on page 79	Map visualizations Map×V; Locations×V(×V...)	
"Question: What Is in This Text?" on page 81	Text visualizations, including word clouds	

Overall Perceptual Concerns

The strengths and weaknesses of human perception drive much of the design of visualizations. Basic perceptual concepts apply across all visualization types. The term *encoding channel* refers to the ways that an attribute is represented in the visualization. In a bar chart, for example, bar length encodes a value, whereas the textual bar caption encodes the category. Different channels have very different perceptual properties, which can be described in terms of how quickly and accurately a reader can interpret them as well as how much they stand out from each other.

There is a well-known hierarchy of accuracy: overall, readers are faster and more accurate when comparing lengths or positions than area (see Figure 5-5). Roughly, the hierarchy runs from length to arc angle, to area to color hue and intensity (Figure 5-5). All else being equal, then, bar charts (which use length) are likely to be preferable to treemaps, which use area. (To read more on this topic, see the article by Cleveland and McGill cited under "Relevant Articles" on page 84.)

Figure 5-5. Difficulty in comparison increases roughly from left to right: comparing length with a shared baseline and with different baselines, comparing angles, comparing square areas or circular areas, and comparing color. Each of these shows three values in the proportion 5:1:3.

Color is difficult to use effectively. A small number of well-chosen colors can be highly distinguishable, particularly for categorical data, but it can be difficult for users to distinguish between more than a handful of colors in a visualization. Nonetheless, color is an invaluable tool in the visualization toolbox because it is a channel that can carry a great deal of meaning and be overlaid on other dimensions. A number of the visualizations described in this chapter use a color scale, such as heatmaps and choropleths. There are a variety of perceptual effects, such as simultaneous contrast and color deficiencies, that make precise numerical judgments about a color scale difficult, if not impossible. As such, it is vital to choose color palettes with care.

There are other important conventions. Lines should connect things that go together, and in most cases, it should be meaningful to look halfway along a line. Objects in visualizations that are stacked atop each other are typically read as to be summed together: their total area is the sum of the areas of their components (Figure 5-2). This is as true in a stacked bar chart as it is in a treemap. Conversely, when areas are discontinuous—two different bars side by side—the analyst expects the viewer to compare them. Closer-together things are easier to compare than further-apart things; thus, a clustered bar chart suggests that the bars in each cluster should be considered in relation to each other, and then the clusters themselves in relation to one another (Figures 5-3 versus 5-4).

None of the data visualizations in this chapter use a three-dimensional perspective. There is an entire research area dedicated to 3D data—physical structures, bodies, weather systems—and many tools meant to visualize things that truly have three spatial dimensions. In our experience and in the experience of many others, using three dimensions tends to lead to challenges in perception: points in space occlude each other; perspective makes it hard to compare sizes; the extra dimension of depth tends to obscure information. Thus, visualization design principles tend to reserve 3D visualization techniques to tasks that are meant to explore the 3D shape of spatial data.

There are a number of excellent resources on the topic of perception for visualization; see "Further Reading" on page 83.

Question: How Is a Measure Distributed?

In this section, we start with a single variable and look at ways to examine how it is distributed. There are a group of subquestions around distributions. Are there some values that recur? Are there outliers? This first class of visualizations is meant to help us understand the distribution of one or two data columns.

Histogram (Categorical)

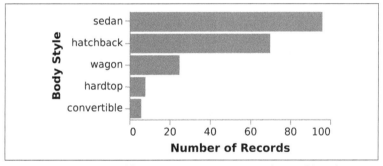

Figure 5-6. Categorical histogram. One categorical variable. This chart shows the distribution of car styles in the cars dataset.

Description
    This is a Categorical × Ratio chart, which can be drawn as a bar chart. Given a list of categorical data, each bar represents the frequency of items in a particular category. Subquestions center around comparing bars: What category has the most, or the fewest, items? Does some category stand out from the others?

Histogram (Quantitative)

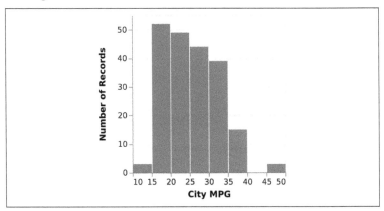

Figure 5-7. Quantitative Histogram. One quantitative variable. This chart shows the distribution of car ratings for the city-mpg field.

Description

A quantitative histogram shows the distribution of a continuous or ordinal variable. It can help identify whether the data is skewed in one direction or another—that is, whether the data is top-heavy or bottom-heavy, or whether there are gaps in the middle of the range or outliers at the end. If there is a small enough number of discrete values, they can be treated as categories. Otherwise, the data is binned into ranges and each range gets its own bar. It is valid for a bin to have no items.

This chart is not really different from the categorical histogram. Fundamentally, it follows the instructions in "Transforming Between Dimension Types" on page 49 to transform a continuous variable into an ordinal one by binning, then aggregating on the count within the bins.

Limitations

The effectiveness of the histogram is based on the effectiveness of the binning. Different choices of bins—varying where the bins start or the bin size—can produce very different-looking results for the same data.

Smoothed Histogram

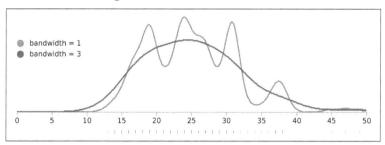

Figure 5-8. Smoothed histogram. One quantitative variable. This plot shows a kernel density estimate of the city-mpg field of the cars dataset. Smoothed with a narrow bandwidth, the dataset shows sharp peaks. Smoothed with a wider bandwidth, the dataset shows a gaussian-like distribution.

Description

A histogram can be smoothed into a continuous curve, known as a *probability distribution function*. Applying a smoothing function implicitly suggests that the underlying data is smooth, and that the data points are a sample drawn from a broader set of possibilities. Like binning functions, smoothing functions are extremely sensitive to parameters and algorithms.

Limitations

The smoothed histogram entirely hides the underlying values, and the y-axis can be difficult for users to interpret. Contrast Figures 5-7 and 5-8, which are drawn with the same data.

Box Plot

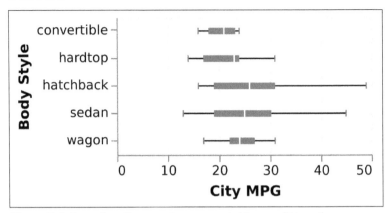

Figure 5-9. Box plot. One continuous variable, conditioned on one or more categorical variables; this chart shows the variation of the city-mpg field, this time across multiple car body styles.

Description

A box plot shows a less detailed summary of a single distribution. At the cost of detail, users can more easily glance at how distributions differ. The box plot family allows you to compare multiple distributions against each other. It can identify such features as the average, standard deviation, and outliers for multiple distributions. Figure 5-9 shows a common use of box plots: to compare one measure across multiple dimensions.

A box plot is computed by choosing series of aggregate values over the distribution—usually the median and the quartiles—for the continuous variable. Other implementations choose instead to render the mean and standard deviations of a distribution.

Limitations

A box plot cannot show multiple peaks or other features of the distribution; it also hides the underlying number of entries. Some box plots can render outliers, although this does not scale to large numbers of points. Other variants, such as the *whisker*, *bean*, and *violin* plots add additional richness to the box plot (see "Further Reading" on page 83).

Density Plot for Two Dimensions

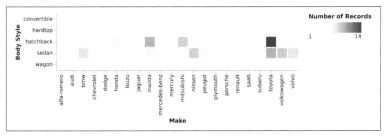

Figure 5-10. Categorical density plot. Two categorical variables. This chart shows the number of cars, grouping body style by make.

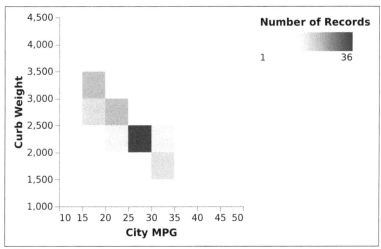

Figure 5-11. Continuous density plot. Two continuous variables. This chart shows the joint distribution of efficiency, as measured in MPG, against the weight of the car.

Description

The density plot shows how two variables change together. Darker spots show places where lots of points occur; lighter spots show places where there are fewer points. Density plots can be used to compare *relative* distributions between two different variables, as well as to find outliers. In the categorical version, it can be used to find how often different pairs of variables go together.

As in a histogram, continuous variables are bucketed. Each cell contains the number of items in which a pair of values co-occur. A density plot may also plot a continuous versus a categorical variable.

Notes

The density plot is a first cousin to the more familiar scatterplot. Where a scatterplot shows individual points, however, a density shows regions. As a result, density plots are far more scalable than scatterplots. At a large number of points, a scatterplot can become a black blob, whereas a density plot can be tuned. Density plots come in many variants, including ones that highlight individual outliers, ones that use smooth curves to show density, and ones that choose non-square binning algorithms (see "Further Reading" on page 83).

Question: How Do Groups Differ from Each Other?

The second major group of questions are those that compare multiple groups. *Are boys taller than girls? Do people buy more chips or soda?* When data values are broken out by categories, the visualizations in this section can show how the values of those categories compare.

Bar Chart

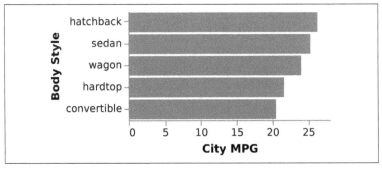

Figure 5-12. Bar chart. One categorical variable, one ordinal. Bar length shows the average efficiency by body style using the same data as in Figure 5-9.

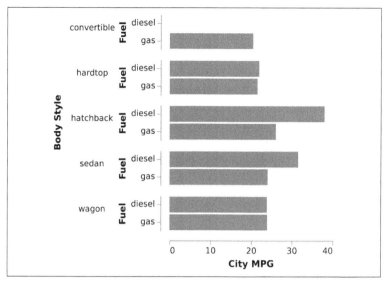

Figure 5-13. Paired (or multiple) series bar chart. One ordinal, two categorical variables. Efficiency by body style is now divided into diesel versus gas cars.

Description

A bar or column chart is a common choice for comparing a single measure per group. A clustered bar chart provides two categories: a major one and a minor one. The task, then, can be more complex: users might compare bars within a cluster or between clusters, or compare the overall shapes of clusters to each other.

The bar chart is useful for comparing values across categories. Users are very good at tasks like mentally sorting bars, identifying extremes, and estimating the average and variance across bars.

Notes

Bars should be ordered in some reasonable order. If the categorical value is based on ordinal data—such as years—then they should be in that order. Otherwise, bars can be ordered from highest to lowest value. In a multiple-view or clustered bar chart, the order should remain consistent.

When a dataset is separated across a categorical variable, each category is sometimes referred to as a *series*; in a multiline chart or a clustered bar chart, each line or bar represents a series.

Limitations

A bar chart begins to be incomprehensible when there are too many categories, except in the case where the bar chart is showing individual values of bucketed, sequential data. If the task is to cluster pairs of bars into groups based on their relative size, then a scatterplot (Figure 5-16) might be a more appropriate tool.

Pie Chart

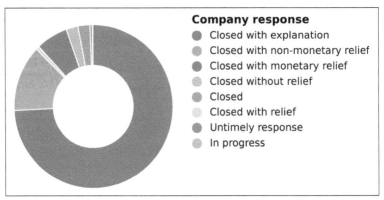

Figure 5-14. Pie (or doughnut) chart. One continuous, one categorical variable. The CFPB data shows the ways that complaints have been closed.

Description

A pie (or doughnut) chart is a variant on a bar chart: it maps wedge angle instead of height to a value. By filling a full 360 degrees around, the pie connotes *parts of a whole*. Pies can be effective for showing certain aspects of the data: *this takes up more than half*, for example. It can be difficult, however, to accurately compare pie wedges to each other unless they are very different in size.

Heatmap

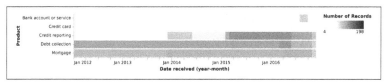

Figure 5-15. Heatmap. Two categorical or continuous variables result in a color variable. The CFPB data shows the number of complaints over time, by product. The data is broken out by month and year.

Description

A heatmap is a two-dimensional analogue to a bar chart: it visualizes the aggregation or value that sits in each bucket. Just as a bar chart is a general mechanism that can be used to render a histogram, the density plot shown in Figure 5-15 is rendered with a heatmap. Many tasks that are carried out with a heatmap might also be fulfilled with a clustered bar chart.

A heatmap allows the user to look across or down the dimensions, looking for commonalities or differences. For example, in Figure 5-15, the user can look across to see patterns in how products are similar or vary, and up to see how company responses vary.

Notes

A heatmap is a first cousin of a density plot, except rather than using merely the count of items, it shows a measure. The term *heatmap* gets used in many contexts; this use is common, but not exclusive. The term can also refer to density plots, for example, and occasionally to treemaps.

Limitations

When a heatmap has many rows or columns, it becomes important to order them to show patterns and trends. Furthermore, dense heatmaps suffer from a host of perceptual problems associated with color, making accurate judgments of individual values sometimes impossible.

Question: Do Individual Items Fall into Groups? Is There a Relationship Between Attributes of Items?

Scatterplots fulfill two sets of closely related tasks. By visualizing items by their attributes, they can help us look at relationships between those attributes or at groupings in the items themselves. *Is there a relationship between height and weight? Do mobile users differ from desktop users with regard to session length or click-through rate?*

Scatterplot

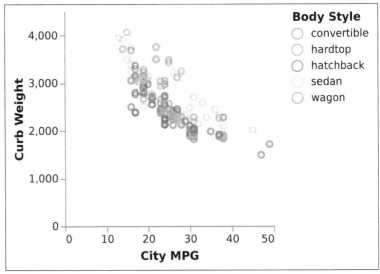

Figure 5-16. Scatterplot. Two continuous variables. Additional continuous, ordinal, or categorical variables can be added for size, color, and shape. This shows the relation between curb weight and MPG for five different styles of car.

Description

A scatterplot places data points on perpendicular axes. The two major axes are used to lay out the points spatially; additional attributes can be used for color, size, or shape.

Scatterplots encourage the user to look at groupings in space. They can identify outliers or groups, such as the points that are in each cluster or the points that are along a main trendline. If the points are colored with an additional categorical variable, then they can address questions about whether different categories behave differently from each other.

Notes

Too many simultaneous encodings will be overwhelming to the reader; colors must be easily distinguishable, and of a small enough number that the reader can interpret them.

Many users find scatterplots difficult to interpret with their two abstract axes. In an infographic, some designers help guide users by highlighting and annotating regions with comments like "People who had high math scores but low written ones," or individual points with comments like "This drink costs $0.50 and has 150 calories."

Limitations

When encoding a third dimension with color or shape, occlusion can get in the way: a user cannot see that a red dot and a blue dot have been drawn in the same place. Also, some tools will draw all of one set of points before they draw any of the next; the reader can be misled by this unintentional bias.

Question: How Does an Attribute Vary Continuously?

Temporal data occurs in almost every context, so line charts are some of the most common forms of charts. *How is a stock, a heart rate, or Twitter traffic doing compared to last month? Is the trend periodic, trending, or noisy?*

Line and Area Charts

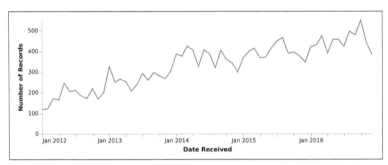

Figure 5-17. Line chart. One ordinal, one continuous variable. This chart shows a count of consumer complaints by year and month for the CFPB data.

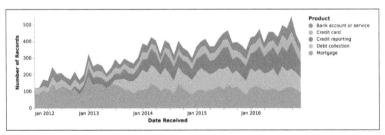

Figure 5-18. Stacked area chart. One ordinal, one continuous, and one categorical variable. This chart shows the count of consumer complaints, like Figure 5-17, but broken out by product. Mortgages stabilized while credit reporting grew (this shows the same data as Figure 5-15).

Description

The line chart family draws a value for each point along a continuous axis. The independent axis is often time, but it can be anything that varies continuously, such as distance. For points that are not in the dataset, the chart shows an interpolated value; a core assumption of a line chart is that the points in between are meaningful and well defined.

A line chart shows change over a continuous variable. That might be a trend (*Profits went up!*) or a repeating pattern (*People read our web page on weekends! This bike ride is hilly!*). Use multiple lines sharing one set of axes to see how multiple sets covary.

A stacked line chart lays multiple lines over each other with the top of one acting as the baseline of the next.

Limitations

In any stacked chart, it can be difficult to see how much the upper layers have changed. In Figure 5-18, for example, the spike in the bottom green layer in January 2013 makes it appear that all categories spiked.

Question: How Are Objects Related to Each Other in a Network or Hierarchy?

Networks and hierarchies help track the connections between items. *Is this person connected to that one? Does this online group have an internal structure? How many people are in this reporting structure? Which product line is selling best?*

Node-Link View

Figure 5-19. Node-link view. A relational variable, in which pairs of data values are linked to each other, plus additional metadata on the nodes and edges. This data from the Les Miserables dataset shows coappearance in the novel between characters. The network has been truncated to 40 nodes for legibility.

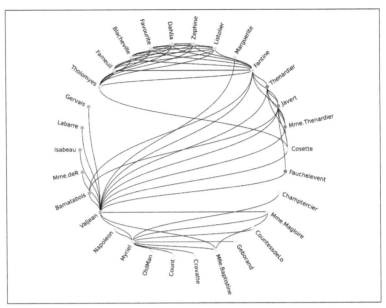

Figure 5-20. Circular network layout. A relational variable, in which pairs of data items are linked to each other, plus additional metadata on the nodes and edges. This shows the same data as Figure 5-19.

Description

    A node-link view draws nodes representing data items, and lines representing links between them. In a force-directed layout such as Figure 5-19, nodes and lines are placed so that connected nodes are nearer each other, while nodes that are not directly connected are further apart; these views help users identify clusters of interconnected nodes. A circular layout like Figure 5-20 maintains an ordering between nodes.

Node-link diagrams are good for understanding connection. A user may be able to pick out well-connected nodes, as well as identify clusters of nodes and isolates. In an ordered circular layout, it is easier to see similar nodes have similar patterns of connection. When an additional dimension is shown using color or shape, tracking *homophily*—whether well-connected nodes are similar with respect to the additional dimension—becomes possible

Limitations

Node-link views are effective for showing only small networks. Researchers have found that the most successful node-link diagrams showed small networks with no more than 10–50 nodes and 20–100 links. At this scale, node-link diagrams are good at showing the overall structure of a sparse graph, although density has a strong impact on readability—a highly connected graph can lead to what's known as a *hairball*. A very few, far larger networks visualized using node-link views have been successful in presenting the general shape of the network. (See "Further Reading" on page 83.)

Rendering node-link view layouts is a research field in its own right, based on what types of tasks will be supported by the visualization. Consider aggregating groups of nodes together to see relationships between them, or providing a drilldown into regions.

Adjacency Matrix

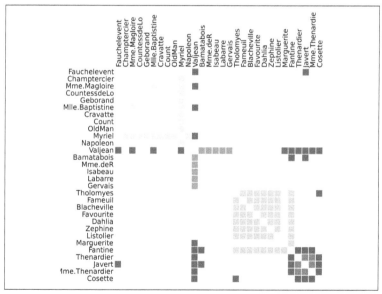

Figure 5-21. Adjacency matrix. A relational variable, in which pairs of data items are linked to each other, plus an additional metadata field mapped to color for the edges. This chart shows the same data as Figures 5-19 and 5-20

Description

    An adjacency matrix shows the connections between data items in a heatmap, where the measure is whether a pair of items are connected.

    The adjacency matrix shows connection between pairs directly; each cell represents an edge. Identifying whether a pair of items is connected is a straightforward task, but pathfinding is more difficult. In addition, with an appropriate ordering, cliques and near-cliques become visible.

Notes

    An adjacency matrix can be more difficult for novices to understand than a node-link diagram. For smaller and sparser networks, a node-link diagram is almost always better. Detecting patterns is very order-dependent; much research has been done on ordering the cells in a matrix in order to bring out patterns.

    Adjacency matrices are not a particularly compact representation; the fairly small matrix in Figure 5-21 still takes up a large amount of space.

Tree View

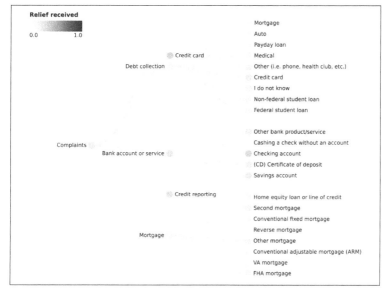

Figure 5-22. Tree view. One hierarchical set of dimensions, perhaps coded with one or two other dimensions (both nodes and edges can be colored and sized). This is a hierarchy of the types of complaints to the CFPB and the percentage of them that received relief. The second layer of the tree corresponds to the values in Figures 5-1 through 5-4.

Description

A tree view uses a node-link diagram to draw a hierarchy. The color of nodes and edges, as well as the thickness of edges, can be mapped to additional dimensions of the dataset. As such, a tree view is good for looking for individual items buried in a hierarchy that are unusual in size or color.

Notes

When trees get large, it can be difficult to pick out individual nodes. In interactive systems, it can be convenient to collapse subtrees together into abstracted nodes, and to elide nodes toward the roof. This sort of *level of detail* interaction allows users to more easily navigate the tree.

Treemap and Sunburst

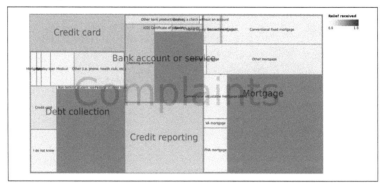

Figure 5-23. Treemap. A hierarchical value, associated with a size and a color for each leaf node. Non-leaf nodes do not get their own colors. This represents the same data as Figure 5-22 but adds a second dimension for size: the number of complaints.

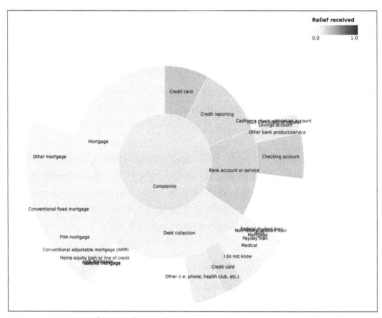

Figure 5-24. Sunburst plot. A hierarchical value, associated with a size and color for each node, including both leaf and internal nodes. This chart shows the same data and mapping as Figure 5-23.

Description

Treemaps and sunburst plots look at relative sizes of things in a hierarchy. For example, a hard drive has folders that each take up space, subfolders take up fractions of their space, and so on. Similarly, a company might organize its products in a hierarchy (categories of products, divided into individual products, divided into editions). Each node is associated with both a size and a color. As with the tree view, color can be mapped to a value or category, but it is far easier to read the total area than with a tree view.

A sunburst plot can make it harder to compare the size of areas, especially between layers, but easier to compare the depth.

Limitations

It can be difficult to accurately compare relative area in these visualizations, especially for oddly shaped pieces or between different layers.

Question: Where Are Objects Located?

Maps are perhaps the most familiar visualizations: many children grow up playing with map puzzles many years before they encounter their first bar chart. As such, they make familiar reference points to place data. *Which state has the most millionaires? Where are the stores that have sold the most snow shovels?*

Geographical Map

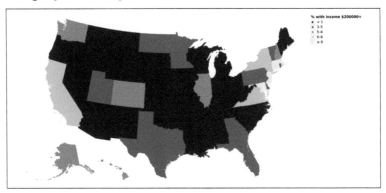

Figure 5-25. Choropleth. Values correspond to regions, such as states or counties. This chart uses census data to look at the percentage of the population with income over $200,000.

Figure 5-26. Dotplot map. A scatterplot, where the x- and y-axes are geographical (or a list of geographical points); additional dimensions for size, color, or shape. Dots are located at the centroid of each zip code; the first digit encodes color.

Description

Geographical visualizations are an entire field in themselves. The choice of choropleth and dotplot here represents just two classic charts from an extremely rich history. Choropleths fill in regions; dotplots place data at points of interest.

Maps can be used for understanding how places vary or are similar, for understanding regional differences, and more.

Notes

One great virtue of maps is that if the audience is reasonably familiar with the area, there is no actual need to label what the space means. Neither Figure 5-25 nor 5-26 has a legend or labels on the states, which is a reasonable omission for people familiar with the geography of the United States.

Limitations

In a choropleth, a great deal of emphasis is given to land area even though size and population are unrelated—a high value in US states like Alaska or Montana (which have a very large area but a low population) might seem more significant than a high value in tiny Rhode Island (which has approximately the same population as Montana, but 1/145 of the land mass).

The spatial distribution of dots in a dotplot is the same, regardless of the dimension being shown with color. For example, most dotplot maps of the United States look somewhat the same: a lot of points on the East Coast, fewer on the West Coast, and fewer still in the center. This is true whether measuring number of millionaires, voters, or sinks sold.

Maps also have the disadvantage that they consume the most powerful encoding channels in the visualization toolbox—position and size—on an aspect that is held constant. This leaves less effective encoding channels like color for showing the dimension of interest.

Question: What Is in This Text?

Visualizing textual data is a common user need. Unfortunately, there is no definitive technique for resolving it. Most approaches fall into the same patterns that are discussed throughout this chapter. They can be found by operationalizing the question further: what is it that the analyst needs to know from the text? Some popular approaches start with counting patterns and frequencies of words or phrases and visualizing these patterns in line charts, bar charts, networks, and so on. There are many subtleties with regard to recognizing word roots and stemming, choosing what aspects to visualize, and handling a set of words with a very high cardinality.

Word Cloud

Figure 5-27. Word cloud. This is a word cloud of the text of the Preface to this book. Color in this chart is arbitrary.

Description

One popular choice for visualizing text is a word cloud. A word cloud is, at heart, something like a bar chart: entities are sized to their counts. It relaxes constraints on position and color, which then get assigned with fairly arbitrary layout algorithms. A word cloud allows the reader to understand the relative frequency of words, and roughly identifies the top handful of words.

Limitations

Perceptually, a word cloud can be challenging: long words, and letters with ascenders and descenders, can make size difficult to estimate. It might be more effective—if less visually interesting —to simply print a bar chart of word frequency.

Conclusion

This chapter has examined several major classes of visualizations. There are a set of shared encoding channels: the placement of items (spatial), color, size. There are also a number of perceptual rules used to help enhance the degree to which visualizations bring out distinctions in questions.

This ties back to the process of operationalization by linking the question to user needs. For example, imagine an analyst who wishes to create a visualization showing that stores in region A are more likely to sell blue jeans than stores in region B. The question that the data counseling process suggests to ask is, "What would it look like to show this?"

The analyst might decide to group stores together by region and show the sum of jeans sold, or the proportion of products. They might decide to plot them on a map. In the former case, they lose granularity (data on individual stores) at the gain of seeing overall trends. Plotting has the opposite effect: it may be hard to see trends against bigger population patterns.

Further Reading

The basic chart types are one of the most well-studied and explored areas of data visualization. This section highlights a (very) few core books:

Bertin, Jacques. *Semiology of Graphics: Diagrams, Graphs, Maps,* trans. William J. Berg (Redlands, CA: ESRI Press, 2010).

- Jacques Bertin's seminal volume is a dense and challenging read (and the English translation is imperfect). However, the work is a treasure trove. Bertin lays out the principles of good information design based on cartography, typography, color theory, and perception. He then walks through, in great detail, the advantages and disadvantages of different chart representations of datasets with qualitative, quantitative, and spatial data types.

Few, Stephen. *Information Dashboard Design: Displaying Data for At-a-Glance Monitoring* (Sebastopol, CA: O'Reilly, 2006).

- Stephen Few takes an opinionated approach to creating information dashboards. In this book, he lays out basic principles of what makes for a good information dashboard. His notes apply both to the individual charts discussed in this chapter and the multiple views in Chapter 6.

Wilkinson, Leland. *The Grammar of Graphics* (Mew York: Springer, 1999).

- This book expresses a particular sequence of creating visuals by mapping from data through geometric primitives and placing them on scales. These core insights make it easy to generalize many visualization techniques and have influenced visualization systems from Tableau, to the *ggplot* package in R, to Vega.

Meirelles, Isabel. *Design for Information.* (Beverly, MA: Rockport Publishers, 2013).

- Trained as a designer, Isabel Meirelles presents the history and best practices for understanding, critiquing, and creating visualizations from a design perspective.

Steele, Julie and Noah Illinski. *Designing Data Visualizations* (Sebastopol, CA: O'Reilly, 2011).

- This is a useful guide to core visualizations, with a stronger emphasis on how to design and present visualizations.

Munzner, Tamara. *Visualization Analysis and Design* (Natick, MA: AK Peters/CRC Press, 2014).

- This textbook is an overview of the state of the art of the data visualization field. It covers data abstraction, provides perceptual guidelines, and discusses faceting into multiple views. Many topics in this book were influenced by Munzner's approach.

Relevant Articles

Cleveland, William S. and Robert McGill. "Graphical Perception: Theory, Experimentation, and Application to the Development of Graphical Methods." *Journal of the American Statistical Association* 79 (1984): 531–554.

- This brief and readable journal article builds a hierarchy of core perceptual tasks in visualization. Its insight is that comparing length is the core perceptual task of a bar chart, whereas comparing angle is core to a pie chart. Comparing these two perceptual tasks can help evaluate the difficulty of understanding a visualization.

Wickham, Hadley and Lisa Stryjewski. "*40 Years of Boxplots*," technical report from had.co.nz (2012)

- This paper (*http://vita.had.co.nz/papers/boxplots.html*) provides an invaluable overview of different box plot variants, including the bean and violin plots, as well as 2D analogues.

Sarikaya, Alper and Michael Gleicher. "Scatterplots: Tasks, Data, and Designs." *IEEE Transactions on Visualization and Computer Graphics* 28 (2018).

- This paper (*https://alper.datav.is/publications/scatterplots*) discusses several major variants of scatterplots and density plots.

Ghoniem, Mohammed, Jean-Daniel Fekete, and Philippe Castagliola, "On the Readability of Graphs Using Node-Link and Matrix-Based Representations: a Controlled Experiment and Statistical Analysis." *Information Visualization* 4 (2005): 114–135.

- This paper explores the readability challenges around large and high-density node-link diagrams for low-level tasks like finding nodes, edges, and paths between nodes.

Datasets

Copies of the data used in this chapter (in both pre-processed and raw form), along with Vega and VegaLite code to create the visualizations in this chapter and in Chapter 6, can be found on the book's website (*https://resources.oreilly.com/examples/0636920041320*). The datasets used are:

CFPB
   The CFPB Consumer Complaint Data (*https://catalog.data.gov/dataset/consumer-complaint-database*) about financial products and services. The dataset is made available on Data.gov, with data as of September 26, 2015.

Cars
   The Automobile dataset (*https://archive.ics.uci.edu/ml/datasets/Automobile*) is based on the 1985 Ward's Automotive Yearbook, courtesy of the UCI Machine Learning Repository (*http://archive.ics.uci.edu/ml/index.php*).

Les Miserables
   This dataset, showing character coappearance in Victor Hugo's *Les Miserables*, first appeared in Donald E. Knuth's *The Stan-*

ford GraphBase: A Platform for Combinatorial Computing (Addison-Wesley, 1993). It is available from the UCI Network Data Repository (*http://bit.ly/2AE1QyI*).

Zip code

The zip code dataset was composed from US Census Bureau data by CivicSpace Labs, and is available for download from Tom Boutell's website (*https://boutell.com/zipcodes/*).

Census

The census data (*http://bit.ly/2A0SZWI*), aggregated at the state level and examining total household income, is available from American FactFinder (US Census).

CHAPTER 6

Multiple and Coordinated Views

The previous chapter provided a gallery of single-chart visualizations. This chapter brings those views together into interactive, connected visuals called *multiple linked views* (MLVs). An MLV leverages multiple visualizations by linking the information shown in each view to the others through user interactions.

MLVs are vital to understanding large and complex data. They allow many different attributes to be viewed at once by splitting them up across a set of views and partitioning the data items to find interesting trends. They can be designed to help guide a user toward the most interesting data items, to show multiple perspectives on data, or to allow the user to dive more deeply into a dataset. In an MLV system, a dataset is shown in multiple simple visualizations, with the data items shown in the different charts corresponding to each other. The charts in each visualization can be used to highlight, control, or filter the data items shown in the others.

There are a number of well-defined MLV design patterns, each of which supports a different set of analysis tasks. This chapter covers five of the best-known patterns: small multiples, scatterplot matrices (SPLOMs), overview+detail, multiform views and dashboards, and overlays. Small multiples and SPLOMs are series of small visualizations that use the same view but show different parts of the data. Overview+detail pairs two views, one as an overview of the complete dataset and the other as a detailed view of a subset of the data. Multiform views and dashboards use different types of visualizations with each view optimized for a subset of attributes. Lastly, overlays are multiple visualizations drawn on a common, shared axis.

This chapter discusses appropriate tasks and provides examples for each of these. There are characteristic interactions that go with most of these design pattern. The chapter describes the ways that users might interact with these visualizations. Table 6-1 provides an overview.

Table 6-1. The design space of multiple linked views

MLV type	Supported task	Data	Interaction	What is shared
Small multiples	Understand and identify differences between subsets or measures of the data	Each view shows a partitioned subset, or a different measure, of the data	Usually static	Different data, same attributes, same view; or, same data, different attributes, same view
SPLOM	Understand relationships and correlation between the attributes	Each scatterplot shows all of the data items for every pair of attributes	Brushing and linking highlights the same data items in different views	Same data, different attributes, same view
Multiform views and dashboards	Understand relationships and correlation between the attributes	Each view shows all of the data items, but different attributes	Brushing and linking highlights the same data items in different views	Same data, different attributes, different views
Overview +detail	Find interesting data items and understand those in detail	Large datasets where all data items and attributes cannot easily be shown at once	Selection in overview; navigation in detail	Same data, different attributes, different views
Overlay	Compare two datasets that share a common attribute	Different, but joinable, datasets	Usually static	Different data, shared attribute, shared axis

Small Multiples

The small multiples design pattern—sometimes also called a *trellis chart*—focuses on showing subsets of a dataset, meaningfully partitioned. The pattern allows an analyst to quickly look across these subsets and compare them in order to find trends, patterns, and outliers.

This pattern is common in everyday interfaces. In online shopping sites, a search query is presented as a grid. In this grid, the results are partitioned based on specific products, and each individual view in the grid gives quick information about what the product looks like, its price, and its rating. Similarly, weather forecasts typically show forecasts for several days with small multiples. Here, the forecast data is partitioned by day; each individual view shows information about the day's temperatures, cloud cover, and precipitation. The layout supports quick skims down the views to get a sense of how the weather will change over the course of the days.

The views in a small multiple must maintain *consistency*, so it is easy to read down or across each individual view to directly compare the data subsets across each attribute. Maintaining the same view of the data while varying the data items is a hallmark of small multiples.

A small-multiples display shows the same visualization repeated across a row, column, or grid of views. Small multiples come in two variants: they can be split by dimension, or they can show differing measures. When a visualization has been split by dimension, each individual view is a visualization of the same attributes, but the views show different subsets of the data, split along a partitioning attribute. The partitioning attribute is typically an ordinal or categorical value—as in Figure 6-1—a binned continuous value.

When a visualization shows multiple measures, each individual view shows most of the same attributes for all the data. Each individual view varies one dimension or measure from its neighbors. In Figure 6-9, the three views all show the same dimensions, but vary on the measure: population, engineers, and hurricanes per state.

Small multiples are particularly good for supporting *comparison* of subsets of the data *across* several attributes of interest—words such as these in an operationalized task point to a small multiples design pattern. For example, the small multiples of choropleth maps in Figure 6-1 support comparison of the percentage of the population in states in the US across different salary ranges.

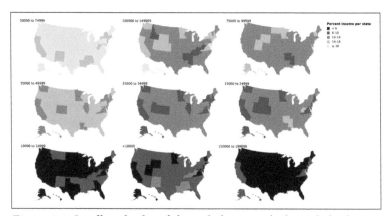

Figure 6-1. Small multiples of choropleths. In each choropleth, the percentages of the states' populations for a specific salary range are shown—the small multiple views are partitioned over the set of salary ranges.

In Figure 6-1, percentage and geographic location are shown in each view, and the data is partitioned by salary range. Each individual view in the small multiples display supports statements like "The state of Alaska has a comparatively lower percentage of residents in the lowest salary range." The full display supports statements like "California and Virginia stand out for their unusual distribution of salary at both the lowest and highest ranges."

One virtue of a small multiples view that is split by dimension is that all the views share the same spatial placement and the same color scale. The shared color scale is useful here because the multiple visualizations have the same meaning. The reader learns to interpret that *yellow* means a high percentage while *purple* is low, and can then effectively look across the charts to compare a specific color, pattern, or spatial location.

Often it is not obvious from a task which attributes should partition versus define the views, and trying different combinations can be useful. It is often fruitful to explore different small multiples during the early EDA stages to not only help in understanding the data, but also enable further refinement of the operationalization.

Conditioning and Generative Grammars

The concept of *conditioning* on a variable cuts across many visualization types. This is the statistical term for partitioning one attribute by another. Any single-view visualization can be changed into a small multiples view by conditioning on one or two dimensions; many visualizations can be overlaid by choosing another color to represent conditioning on a second dimension.

A bar chart is a small multiple of single bars, partitioned on an attribute. A clustered bar chart is a hierarchy of small multiples within a small multiples display. This sort of logic drives *The Grammar of Graphics*, which reduces every point on a visualization to a mark drawn in a particular way as described by the data; tools like *ggplot* and Vega explore this philosophy further. See "Further Reading" on page 83.

Scatterplot Matrices

Scatterplot matrices (SPLOMs) are related to small multiples in that they use the same visualization—a scatterplot—across a matrix layout. Instead of showing subsets of data items across a few choice attributes, as in a small multiples display, they instead show the *complete* dataset in a matrix of scatterplots. More specifically, a SPLOM pairs each (usually) continuous numeric attribute against every other attribute in a (diagonally symmetric) matrix layout of scatterplots (Figure 6-2). As with other scatterplots, as discussed in Chapter 5, items in the scatterplot may also be colored and sized by additional attributes.

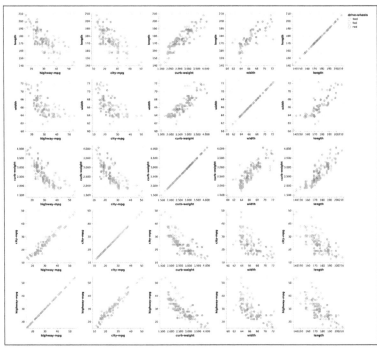

Figure 6-2. A SPLOM comparing attributes of cars in the scatterplots, with a color encoding indicating whether the cars are all-, rear-, or front-wheel drive. This chart helps show, for example, that rear- and front-wheel-drive cars can be separated by their curb weight in conjunction with city-mpg or highway-mpg more than by their width and length.

A SPLOM is primarily useful for characterizing relations between attributes in the earliest stages of EDA. Finding these relationships can help in narrowing down which attributes may be of most interest for further study during later EDA stages.

Overview+Detail

The overview+detail design pattern is essential for navigating and exploring large datasets in order to find interesting data items. It applies to any dataset that is too big—in terms of the number of data items, the number of attributes, or both—to show all at once. This design pattern includes an *overview* visualization that helps in finding interesting subsets of the data, and a linked *detail view* that shows the low-level attribute values associated with the selected subsets. Words in a task such as *locate* and *find* may indicate an overview+detail design pattern.

This design pattern is common in email clients, which provide an overview of the inbox showing the sender, subject, and date for all emails. Selection of an email in this overview then triggers a detailed email view to show the complete contents of the message. This is a flexible, user-driven process that supports a number of tasks: reading new emails, finding emails sent last night, or going back to a specific topic from yesterday, to name a few. The overview pane gives just enough information to make the selection, which is then shown in its entirety in the detail view. This detail view updates with each new selection.

Overview+detail is also frequently used as a navigation aid to provide context for movement around virtual spaces, such as maps, video games, or images. For example, Figure 6-3 is a screenshot from a photo viewing application. The overview is a small, contextual view that supports panning and zooming; the detail view shows a zoomed, detailed portion of the photo.

Figure 6-3. Some photo-viewing apps support overview+detail for panning and zooming an image. Here, the overview in the bottom-right corner indicates which part of the image is being shown in the larger detail view.

The overview+detail design pattern supports guided navigation to help find interesting subsets of the data. This pattern looks across many data items, using either one or several attributes as a measure of *interestingness*. The overview may use an attribute that is shown in other views, or a new, summarizing metric created from the underlying data. A selection in the overview triggers an update in the detail view to show the underlying details about the selected subset. This is typically a one-way interaction where selection in the overview drives what is shown in the detail view, but not vice versa.

What makes for *interestingness*? It is any attribute that helps figure out what subsets are worth looking at in the dataset. If the analyst is looking for places where data has extreme values, for example, it might be the count of items in that area, the maximum value of an attribute, or the average. It might be a synthetic value, such as an anomaly score. The case study in Chapter 8 has an overview that uses a distance function to help guide users to the most interesting bits of detail.

Figure 6-4 shows a dataset of genes located within a chromosome.[1] There are thousands of genes, far too many to reasonably show in a single view. Instead, the overview on the left shows *regions of interest*, each of which contains a set of related genes, shown as colored bars along the chromosome. These bars can be selected, triggering the detail view on the right. This detail view shows the individual genes within the selected region.

---

1 This visualization tool is discussed in "MizBee: A Multiscale Synteny Browser." (*http:// doi.ieeecomputersociety.org/10.1109/TVCG.2009.167*) See "Further Reading" on page 104.

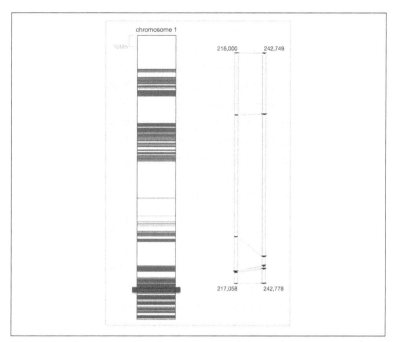

Figure 6-4. Overview+detail views in a tool for exploring genetic data. The overview on the left shows regions of interest, color-coded based on a similarity function. Selecting a region of interest triggers the detail view on the right to show the location of individual genes within the selected region.

Overviews and details can nest for larger and more complex datasets. Figure 6-4 is actually part of a larger system that has two levels of overview to support looking across complete genomes—this system is shown in Figure 6-5. This visualization tool, called MizBee, supports selection of chromosomes of interest in the left view, regions of interest in the middle view, and detailed analysis of genes in the right view. A video of this system in action can be found on the book's website (*https://resources.oreilly.com/examples/ 0636920041320*).

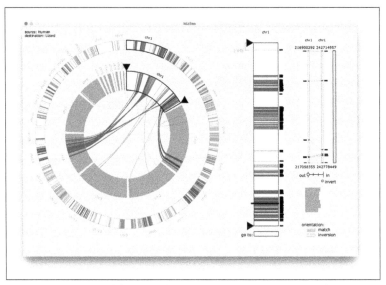

Figure 6-5. This tool for visualizing comparative genomics data has two levels of overview. Selecting a chromosome in the overview on the left triggers a more detailed overview of the selected chromosome in the middle view. In this middle view, regions of interest are selected to then trigger low-level details about individual genes in the detail view on the right.

Overview+detail supports open-ended exploration across the complete dataset and is useful for helping a user build a mental model of what is interesting within a dataset and what more detailed relationships should be explored. Choosing a good proxy for interestingness is essential to an effective overview+detail—oftentimes, the overview is designed to support a range of metrics that the user can switch between dynamically. It is often later in the process that a good understanding of what is interesting emerges. Furthermore, developing overview+detail tools typically requires some significant programming, making them somewhat heavyweight for early EDA. These tools are often developed later in the process, and often serve as the final visualization design.

Multiform Views and Dashboards

A single view can usually only effectively show three or four attributes. When trying to determine how multiple attributes are related to each other, then, a multiform linked visualization can show the connections between multiple attributes. A multiform visualization shows attributes across multiple visualizations, each tailored to most effectively show a small subset of the attributes. In this design pattern, no one view is best or primary and any one view by itself is insufficient.

Each view shows all of the data items, but just a portion of the data attributes. The views themselves are each designed to be most effective for showing one or a few of the attributes, and many views can be shown at once to support finding patterns, trends, and correlations across many attributes. Instead of primarily supporting characterization of patterns in the *data items*, like a small multiples visualization, a multiform visualization supports characterization of patterns in the *attributes*.

This design pattern uses an interaction technique called *brushing and linking*, where selecting data items in one view triggers highlighting of those selected items in the other views, supporting fine-scale analysis of relationships across the attributes.

For example, in Figure 6-6 the view on the left is showing 2D spatial locations for each data item, with a metric encoded at each point, using color. We know from Chapter 5 that color is relatively ineffective for precisely comparing quantitative values; thus, the linked bar chart view on the right shows the metric for each data point using spatial encoding (height). The views are linked such that when the mouse hovers over a data item in the left view, the corresponding bar is highlighted in the right view—the interaction can be viewed in the video on the book's website (*https://resources.oreilly.com/examples/0636920041320*).

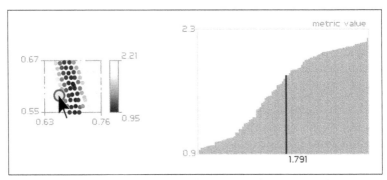

Figure 6-6. In this multiform visualization, both views are showing the same attribute across all the data items. On the left, that attribute is encoded with color, along with the spatial location of each data item. To overcome the perceptual challenges of making fine-scale comparisons of the attribute values using color, the linked view on the right encodes the attribute using a bar chart. The two views are linked together with brushing.

A multiform visualization such as this can give users access to a broad set of attributes across the complete dataset, making it particularly useful in the middle of the data counseling process.

Dashboards are a type of multiform visualization used to summarize and monitor data. These are most useful when proxies have been well validated and the task is well understood. This design pattern brings a number of carefully selected attributes together for fast, and often continuous, monitoring—dashboards are often linked to updating data streams. While many allow interactivity for further investigation, they typically do not depend on it. Dashboards are often used for presenting and monitoring data and are typically designed for at-a-glance analysis rather than deep exploration and analysis. An example of a business dashboard is shown in Figure 6-7.

Figure 6-7. This sample business intelligence dashboard represents a number of different measures and dimensions of a dataset: single numbers summarize important features; scatterplots, bar charts, line charts, and maps address specific tasks. The cells are linked together: choosing a specific element in one panel acts as a filter or highlight against the others.

Overlays

A final MLV design pattern, overlays, uses a shared coordinate system to orient views together—these views are similar in that they share a common coordinate system, but could be different in the visualization type they use. This variation makes it easy to find patterns and trends among a small number of attributes along a common attribute, such as time or space. This form often occurs with geospatial and temporal data; the weather map in Figure 6-8 is an example. In this visualization, three different attributes are layered in the same view: temperature using color, pressure using isolines (contours), and wind speed and direction using wind-barb icons. All three attributes are using the same coordinate system, namely geospatial location over the continental United States. By visualizing these three attributes together, it is easier to make inferences about relationships between them.

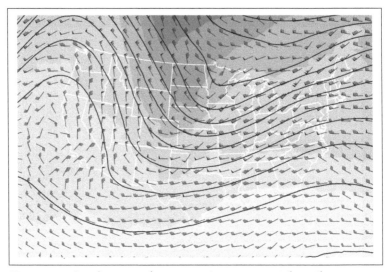

Figure 6-8. Overlays are often seen using a geospatial attribute as a common axis. In this weather map, temperature, pressure, and wind speed are overlaid on a map of the United States.

Besides comparing attributes, overlays are also good for saving pixels and presenting more information in a single display more compactly. On the other hand, they can add more visual complexity. Making detailed judgments about the weather attributes in Figure 6-8 requires a fair amount of attention—too much detail in an overlay can overwhelm a user quickly. Interaction can help with visual clutter, such as highlighting a specific layer of the overlay when a label in the legend is rolled over. In general, overlays are a great option when your analysis requires a small set of attributes to compare and the shared coordinate system is familiar.

Axis Alignment and Scale Consistency

One important aspect of all of these forms of multiple visualizations is finding and aligning shared axes. In general, if two different parts of a visualization are meant to show the same scale, they should be aligned and sized the same way. In a small multiple view of histograms, for example, ensuring that the bins are consistent among the histograms makes it far easier for the user to compare bins to each other. Similarly, when overlaying several series with different ranges, it is worth considering whether the percentage change is most important, which would allow for a common y-axis.

The principles of alignment and consistency play into Figure 6-9, which illustrates the value of maintaining consistent axes while showing independent color scales. The three maps show very different data—the population, percentage of the population that are engineers, and number of hurricanes. The shared coordinate system and aligned axes help the reader compare the maps; the different color palettes emphasize that the attributes, scales, and meaning are very different between the three charts.

Figure 6-9. These three choropleths illustrate the value of aligning scales and maintaining coordinate systems. The maps show the population of each state, the percentage of the population that are engineers, and the number of hurricanes. (The very different map styles suggest that engineers do not cause hurricanes.)

Interacting with Multiple Linked Views

Many of these MLV design patterns support the concept of linking views by interacting with the data. The role of linked-view interactions is to select data in one view that is then reflected in another view, using the data as a selector. This is broadly referred to as *brushing and linking.*

The concept of brushing and linking brings together two subtly different types of interaction intentions: cross-highlighting and cross-filtering. For example, in a SPLOM it is common to select data items in one of the scatterplots to see how they are reflected in others; this is known as *cross-highlighting.* Cross-highlighting can be implemented when individual data points correspond in multiple charts.

Cross-filtering means that the selection on one chart removes data items from other charts. It might make sense, instead, to cross-filter on ranges or values of attributes—for example, by dragging along an attribute to mean "all data items with these values along this attribute."

Interestingly, there's little consensus on the exact specification of these two different intentions. Selecting a region can mean filtering to only a set of data items, or it can mean highlighting those points.

Figure 6-10 shows a cross-selection tool in action. The dataset (from World Bank Development Data) shows a series of countries, listed by the percentage of their population aged 15–64, and the percentage over 64. A scatterplot on the right side plots these two numbers against each other. The user has made a selection within the scatterplot; this highlights the corresponding data in both the lists.

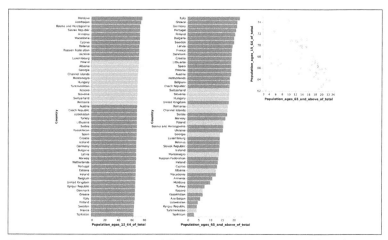

Figure 6-10. Cross-selection. The three views—two sorted bar charts and a scatterplot—are linked together. The user has selected a region of the scatterplot (grey box, orange dots), and the selected values correspondingly light up on the bar charts. This is based on the World Bank dataset.

MLVs and the Operationalization Process

The different types of MLVs tend to be useful at different stages in the operationalization process.

The SPLOM tends to be used early. It is designed to help an analyst dig around in an unfamiliar dataset, or to look at lots of different attributes and see whether there are any interesting correlations between them. SPLOMs are usually an exploratory tool, used when a user can't yet decide which dimensions will make good partitions or measures. It can help clarify the nature of the data and identify which dimensions will be interesting to visualize and explore.

Similarly, small multiples are a good way to rapidly scan how subsets of the data items compare to each other across several attributes. They are often useful at the early stages but continue to be useful later, when the final task is to compare aspects of the data by a partition.

Interactive multiform views often occur in the middle parts of the operationalization process. Brushing and linking between two views can help identify the parts of the data where interesting phenomena occur. The middle part of analysis is also where overview+detail visualizations are helpful—when you know enough about the data to be able to identify an *interestingness* measure and can use it to more richly explore the details of individual data items. Overlays are great here too, when it is known which few attributes are likely to be most important.

At the end of the operationalization, a dashboard is often the result of relentless pruning of ideas for proxies. Having examined the attributes and their interactions, the user now knows which proxies are useful for answering questions, and which attributes are most important. It begins to make sense to create multiple visualizations for different tasks. Each highly curated visualization helps to answer a definite and specific question.

Conclusion

Multiple linked views are design patterns that provide important support for making sense of complex and large datasets. Breaking up the data across multiple views avoids overwhelming a user with extremely dense visualizations, and also allows for optimization of each view based on the characteristics of the underlying data and task.

These design patterns are often used in conjunction with each other. Chapter 7 uses a variety of different visuals, with interactive linking between an overview-and-detail and a series of overlays. Similarly, Chapter 8 illustrates an example of an MLV system that combines an overview+detail with small multiples, small multiples with overlays, and a two-level overview flow.

Further Reading

Meyer, Miriah, Tamara Munzner, and Pfister Hanspeter. "MizBee: A Multiscale Synteny Browser." *IEEE Transactions on Visualization and Computer Graphics* 15 (2009): 897–904. This paper describes the MizBee system, which combines the overview+detail pattern with small multiples, overlays, and multiform views in a single tool to address a series of tasks in biology.

Datasets

In addition to the datasets in Chapter 5, this chapter also uses:

World Bank development data
    Data from the World Bank about development indicators of countries, compiled from officially recognized international sources' World Statistics eXplorer (*http://bit.ly/2B0VD2k*).

CHAPTER 7

Case Study 1: Visualizing Telemetry to Improve Software

The previous chapters of this book explore the data counseling process: how to move from an ambiguous question to a more precise one, and how to refine a design through iteration into a final visualization. This description, however, has missed some of the twists and turns in the data counseling process. Data counseling goes through a series of iterations, each of which casts new light on the questions, but encounters dead ends. Ideas that seem insightful in a sketch turn out not to scale, or are not interpretable when used with real data. At each of these steps, the goal itself may change as new aspects come to light.

To see how this process can evolve in the real world, this chapter reviews a case study from a team that Danyel worked with at Microsoft. To protect sensitive information, this study obfuscates some images and details slightly. In addition, this telling reduces some of the complexity.

Introduction

One of Danyel's roles at Microsoft is to consult with teams from the rest of the company about visualization. Jacqueline, who works on a data science team, emailed him a question: "How would we show distributions so that they pop for users?"

It can be hard to answer such a question without more context. What sort of distributions? Are they based on data, or are they abstract functions? What aspects of them should pop out? For example, Jacqueline might want to let her users see whether a given distribution is close to an expected distribution, or whether it has outliers. The designer does not yet have enough information to figure out what sort of visualization to create.

In some cases, hearing this sort of low-level question can be a sign that a team has reached a dead end. The goal in data counseling is to help them work back out—to discover what their real need is and then operationalize a visualization that helps with that.

Project Background

Danyel and Jacqueline discussed her question in a first data counseling interview. The goal of the interview was to learn more about the real question: who is going to look at these distributions and what do they want to decide? In this case, Jacqueline's team was not stuck. She had assembled a data science team with a clear notion of the problem they wanted to solve. Her team was building a tool, and they knew precisely what it was for and who would use it. Their question was instead figuring out the right way to present that information to users.

Their tool was a backend tool meant to support product teams getting ready to ship software to end users. Those product teams are very concerned about customer satisfaction and want to ensure that they ship software their end users will find satisfying.

The product team's high-level goal, then, is: "As we update software versions, show whether new versions are more satisfying to users." Customer satisfaction can be measured through surveys and interviews, and one of the most frequently cited drivers of satisfaction is the speed at which the application runs. Users complain when applications take too long to start up, and studies have shown that users stop using software that feels laggy. As a result, software responsiveness is one proxy for the desired outcome, which is customer satisfaction.

This proxy is used throughout the build and ship process. Software developers and maintainers want to know whether their system is fast enough for end users to enjoy using. Managers want to know which features need more resources to get the product up to a quality bar.

To address these questions, product teams instrument applications to produce telemetry, which monitors end-user actions during the beta process and logs them to the product teams' servers. The telemetry logs show how long operations take, which can be used to figure out the responsiveness of the application.

A product consists of dozens or hundreds of functions, each of which can be instrumented. This team uses the speed of a function as a proxy for its responsiveness.

In Chapter 2, we suggest refining the goal with the proxies. We could rephrase it as "Show whether the responsiveness of the functions within the software improved between versions.'"

Responsiveness is not a single number. If a population of a hundred users uses a piece of software that carries out a single function, their experiences will vary; it will be faster for some than others. One user might be behind a slow network, while another might be on a computer that is having a bad day. Some users will be sitting at new computers connected to fast networks but might ask to do something that takes a lot of server time. The responsiveness of an operation is a distribution across these user experiences. The teams wanted to be able to characterize and distinguish these groups of users.

Jacqueline's analysis team was building tools to analyze these telemetry results. They had a pilot customer who was releasing beta versions of Lync.[1] Lync is a business communications tool that lets users have one-on-one chats and multiparty voice and video calls, as well as share screens, presentations, and notes. It connects to a company directory of users, allowing users to look each other up. The Lync development team, aware that responsiveness would be important, had built in telemetry and logging features. (Some of this case study has also been discussed in another paper; see "Further Reading" on page 124.)

The Lync team was measuring responsiveness for these individual features. In addition, they measured the overall performance for

---

1 Now known as Skype for Business.

scenarios. A *scenario* is a sequence of logically connected features. For example, one scenario might be named "start session," and would consist of features like "connect to server," "authenticate user with server," "check for missed calls," and "populate list of contacts." In this scenario, the analysts might want to be able to say things like "making a connection has improved since the last build, but ending a call is still taking too long."

In describing these proxies in terms of the operationalization, then, we could refine the goal a little further: For each feature and scenario, across different groups of users, is the speed in one build better than in previous builds?

The Data

The raw data is the telemetry, which comes in the form of reports. Each logged report starts with information that applies to a single user and a single session:

```
Location: Redmond
Software Version: 123.4
Platform: 64 bit Windows 7
Running in the Laboratory: No
System Memory: 16 GB
Network Speed: 10 MBpS
...
```

The report then logs events when a user carries out a feature and what scenario it goes with. Each of these is associated with a duration (see Table 7-1).

Table 7-1. Sample of event log

Session ID	Scenario	Feature	Duration (ms)
S1	Startup	Connect to server	300
S1	Startup	Log in	250
S1	Startup	Download contacts	135
S1	Search for user	Search entry box appears	20
...			

Each row in the table represents a single record—the lowest level of the data. The goal refers to various groupings: the distribution of performance by different categories of user, different features and scenarios, and different software versions. Jacqueline wanted to design a system that would offer the Lync team the opportunity to aggregate across different groupings. The analyst should be able to choose to look only at users looking at low-memory systems, or those running Windows 7. Example 7-1 shows how we can break this goal down, following the process in Chapter 2.

Example 7-1. Breaking down the Lync team's task

Task: Compare the duration for carrying out a scenario across different builds and features

Action: Compare

Object: The set of all event records that describe a single feature or scenario

Measure: Duration

Grouping: Build, analyst-selected features

Determining How to Compare Builds

This revised goal is still ambiguous: we do not yet know how to carry out a comparison between two different groups of durations. For two builds, there is a distribution of values representing the speed. The system should have an ability to help the user decide which distribution is better.

Historically, the Lync product team used a dashboard of data, presented as a grid of colored lights; each row in the grid corresponded to one feature, and each feature had a desired responsiveness. The grid showed the percentage of users who got the desired performance, color-coded red, yellow, or green (Figure 7-1). For example, if starting a call should be faster than half a second, and 60% of users had a less responsive experience, then a red dashboard light would warn that starting a call is problematic.

Build				
Feature	1607	1620	1623	1643
Begin chat	●	●	●	●
Send message	◆	◆	△	△
Start screen share	◆	△	△	●
Start phone call	◆	◆	●	●
Send file	◆	△	●	△

Figure 7-1. Sample performance dashboard (sketch). Build numbers are across the top; features scroll down. Green lights indicate features and builds that have acceptable performance for a large percentage of users; red lights indicate those with a smaller percentage (danger) and yellow a middling percentage (caution).

The proxy metric used in this tool is the percentage of sessions that are better than the threshold. This can be problematic. It is entirely possible to make a change that makes some people's experience a little better and others' much worse, but that turns the light from yellow to green. It is hard to drill down into the lights: while a yellow light might show that 20% of sessions see poor performance, is this the same set of users each time or is it randomly distributed? Is it possible to identify which subpopulations are failing? These thresholds strip out much of the richness of the raw data and make it harder to interpret. The team was unsatisfied with the existing proxy: they wanted to bring that richness back in and to help communicate the data to their end users.

This is where Jacqueline brought Danyel in. The existing presentation of the data was hiding its richness. We began to look at some responsiveness data from the telemetry logs, picking out one feature and one build. A histogram of that data can be seen in Figure 7-2. The thick vertical line shows the acceptable performance threshold, at 5,000 ms. The team had been exploring whether a Gaussian curve would approximate the data well, and plotted the best fit with a red curve.

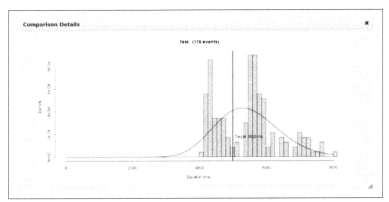

Figure 7-2. *The gray bars are a histogram of connecting to a login server; the red curve is a best-fit Gaussian curve. The vertical black line represents 5,000 ms, the desired threshold for this scenario.*

A number of different insights are quickly visible in this histogram. The first is that this feature always takes at least 4,000 ms. Above that threshold, this histogram seems bimodal. A bimodal curve suggests that there are two different populations here: one group who almost all have a good experience, and a second population who have a poor one. These are the sorts of things that it might be useful to show in the tool because they give a strong cue where to look further.

Seeing the bimodal curve might encourage a user to start figuring out what is different between these two populations, and break them down. Is there a difference between the users who see a 4,000–5,000 ms response, and those who see a 5,000–8,000 ms response? For example, it might be that the longer time represents users who are logged in from a remote network or mobile application. Separating these populations can lead to locating bugs or fixing performance errors in the code.

This also leads to thinking more about the goal of making the software better. Improving responsiveness could have a number of meanings—it could involve shrinking the gap between the two populations or moving the entire distribution leftward. For example, the fact that the minimum time is four seconds suggests that there might be a hardcoded timeout somewhere in the system. Is that true?

Seeing the richness embedded in the data, as in Figure 7-2, convinced all of us that it is critical to let users see the full distribution.

Comparing Distributions to Understand "Better"

With this two-peaked histogram, the team now wanted to allow users to split apart the two peaks and explore different user populations. There are two subtasks:

- For each scenario and feature, characterize how the distribution of speed has changed since previous builds. In what ways has it improved?

- Within a single build, for a given scenario and feature, characterize the distribution of speed. If there are multiple peaks, identify the factors upon which they vary.

These comparisons both suggest grouping the data. The per-session data can help cluster users; they can be grouped by location, or by their system configuration. Similarly, sessions can be divided by software version. As such, a single distribution curve is not enough; we want to see multiple distributions at once. This, then, is where it is important to compare distributions.

Danyel decided to produce a few data sketches to help the team think about what it would look like to compare distributions (see Figures 7-3 and 7-4). As a starting point, he took performance information from two beta builds. These are two fairly similar datasets, enough so that putting them next to each other does not reveal obvious differences. The question was, were there visualizations that would allow analysts to pick them apart?

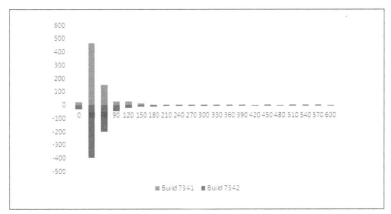

Figure 7-3. A data sketch of a stacked bar chart comparing two distri-butions.

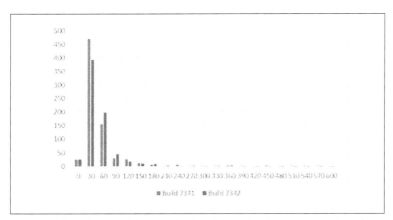

Figure 7-4. A data sketch of a clustered bar chart comparing two dis-tributions.

Neither of these sketches was quite right. The paired bars are diffi-cult to interpret as seeing one distribution requires reading past the other data. The stacked bars make it difficult to read the differences in the curve.

After bringing these sketches to the team, along with several other comparisons, Danyel decided to take a look instead at a smoothed density estimate curve. Smoothed curves highlight differences between the distributions and also take care of the fact that some distributions may have more data than others.

The team liked the smoothed histogram because they felt that the comparison helped users see the data more directly. They decided to adopt the smoothed histogram as one of the core visuals that would appear in their final tool. As seen in Figure 7-5, several features in the final tool compare smoothed histograms directly to each other.

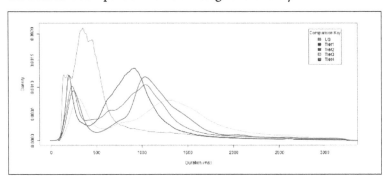

Figure 7-5. A screenshot from a more finished part of the final tool. It provides smoothed curves across different user groups, builds, or conditions.

The next step in the process was to work back upward. The team now had a low-level instrument for comparing sets of distributions, which they would use to compare user groups, builds, and other attributes. We now needed to resolve a broader question: how would users know which distributions were worth examining?

Multiple Scenarios

Jacqueline's team wanted to ensure that the final tool would appeal to release managers. Release managers ensure that all features of the product are ready to ship at the same time, and are responsible for knowing which components will be ready on time. Release mangers worry about trade-offs between features: a server cache that speeds up "look up address" might slow down "confirm user is online." How could they provide release managers with a holistic sense of the entire application?

As Jacqueline explained, release managers have two different tasks with regard to this data:

- Identify which scenarios have (or have not) improved since previous builds and which scenarios have the best (and worst) performance.

- For any given scenario, identify which features are the most problematic.

We used these two tasks to motivate the design for the final tool. It would be based on a dashboard, which would provide an overview of scenarios across multiple builds. Release managers could then zoom in on any scenario to see the constituent features.

Sketching Dashboards

We began a process of searching out and sketching interface designs in between meetings, and sharing and critiquing them during meetings. The goal of the process was to see what interactions and visualizations emerged from the designs and to understand what we wanted to let release managers see.

For example, one team member brought in Figure 7-6 as a possible model. We looked it over as a group. The team felt that the heatmap made for a good overview. They liked the way that it shows that for a number of features (down the left side), multiple versions can be compared (across). While on the surface this is much like the lights grid (Figure 7-1), the important part was the idea of being able to zoom in on the cells.

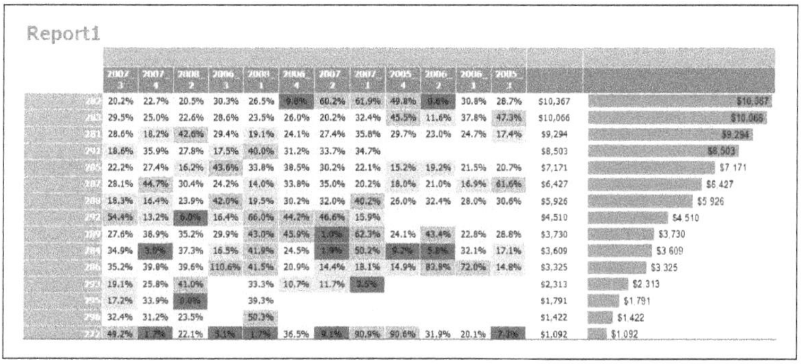

Figure 7-6. Heatmap. The team found this illustration a helpful way to think about the problem despite the fact that it shows sales data.

A different team member noted that there were too many features and scenarios to compare at once, and added a hierarchical component (Figure 7-7). The top-level view shows scenarios but hides lower-level features. This forces the designer to choose a color for

each scenario, even though a scenario is made up of multiple features. In the sketch, each scenario is colored by its worst feature.

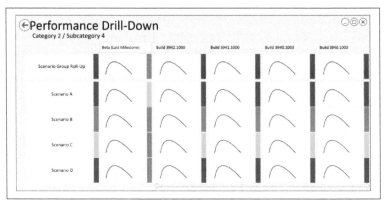

*Figure 7-7. A sketch for the performance dashboard. This lo-fi sketch
helped us think about the hierarchy of data (categories, subcatego-
ries), the necessity for color-coding, and a possible way to bubble performance histograms to the surface.*

The team began to iterate on the sketches. Figure 7-8 was an attempt
to show a set of metrics: whether the scenario passes or fails is mapped to color, success thresholds are drawn with a white bar, and the
histogram (blue) compares scenarios across multiple builds.

Figure 7-8 helped clarify what the group really needed. This sketch
dedicates a lot of horizontal space to past versions; while it is useful
to see how the current version compares to the last one or two, comparing it to more remote history is not a key task. Also, the aggregate task on the right, Scenario (All), is not quite right; there is no
proxy that aggregates multiple scenarios together.

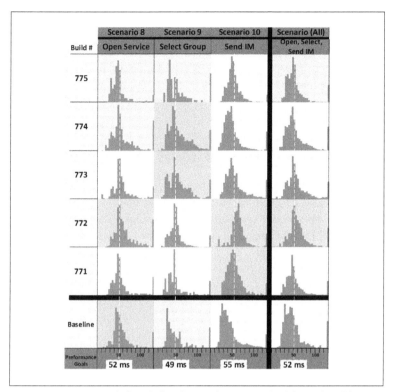

Figure 7-8. A second sketch for the performance dashboard. Adding data sketches indicated the importance of scales and showing thresholds.

The team used these as starting points as they looked at the hierarchical interaction design for their tool.

Turning Back to the Data

Sketching is useful to clarify tasks, but it is very important to come back to the data. The team had begun to converge on a plan—the system would start with a high-level dashboard, which would lead to low-level purpose-built visualizations to compare histograms. As they began to work on incorporating the data into the dashboard, they noticed that in lots of cases, there were far more failures than working cases. In beta versions of the software, calls would sometimes not connect, servers would be disabled, and networks would be disconnected.

Danyel drew a handful of sketches for how to handle failures in a histogram. Failed tests could be marked as taking a lot of time or could be removed from the chart. The team brought these designs back to their prospective users to try to better understand their needs. They learned that in the beta phase, failures were understood differently from responsiveness problems and would only confuse the histogram.

Final UI for High-Level Goals

We combined these ideas to create a single visualization system. The top-level view allowed users to pick a scenario. Once they had selected it, they could see each of the features in Figure 7-9. Each gray box represents a feature; each small dot represents a number of users trying that feature.

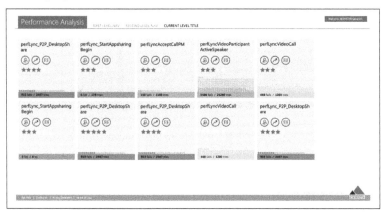

Figure 7-9. The final top-level overview is a scenario and feature selector. Each rectangle represents a single scenario; the colored dots below cue success rates and amount of usage. The three circles on each panel are buttons leading to detailed charts.

Each rectangle show a scenario or feature. The colored bar, dots, and stars all give information about success of the scenario or feature. Each box also contains three circular control buttons. One of the control buttons leads to the histogram for the most recent version, across different user groups (Figure 7-5). Another leads to a comparison tool that allows users to compare populations across multiple builds (Figure 7-10).

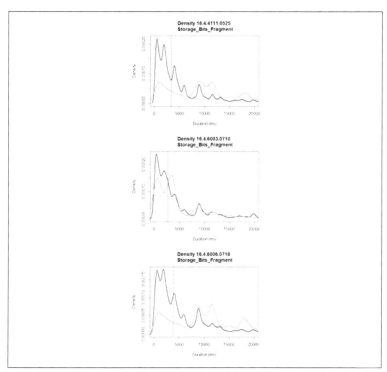

Figure 7-10. Comparing three versions of the software in a detail view, split by two countries.

Figure 7-10 shows an analysis in the tool of performance in two different countries—we'll call them Green and Blue—for three different versions of the software (the newest version is at the bottom). The service has a data center hosted in Blue; as such, most Blue customers experience consistently similar performance. Customers in Green, however, experience very different performance: some users do well, but a great many do poorly. It turns out that the support team receives many support calls from Green customers related to poor and inconsistent performance and that these graphs support their claims.

The middle build seems to show similar curves in Green and Blue—had the team managed to fix the problems here? After studying the data in more detail, they realized that build 0710 was offered only very briefly. As a result, only people with very good network connections—in Green and in Blue—had access to the data, and so only users in Green who had good network connections got the data.

This accidental experiment suggested that the challenge with Green's performance was in handling poor network connections, and the development team began to work on optimizing their system for bad networks. It also made visible, however, that the visualization wasn't showing the number of users as clearly as it should. Seeing that the number of users was way down would have clarified the issue.

Additional Visualizations

The team added additional visualizations to the tool based on other sorts of comparisons. For example, some release managers wanted to see how the software was evolving across many versions and a long development process. The notched bar chart provides both a summary of the number of users and the broad scale of the distribution. In Figure 7-11, for example, there is much more data about build 4420 than about the more recent versions, showing that performance is not obviously improving yet.

As the release teams looked at the tool, they pointed out that geography was turning out to be a major factor for user performance. The team added a visualization of performance by country to help guide searches (Figure 7-12).

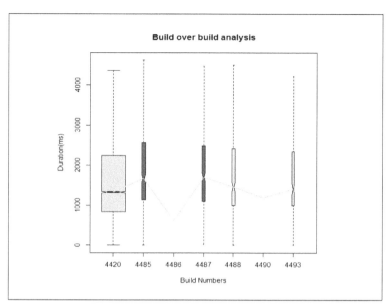

Figure 7-11. A visualization to compare multiple builds. Thickness of the bars is mapped to the number of users of that version; color is mapped to other attributes of the build.

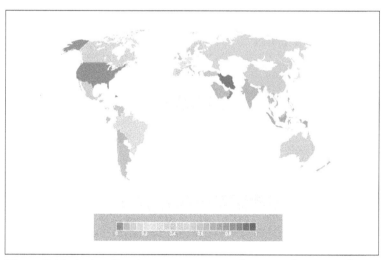

Figure 7-12. A visualization to compare performance by geography, for one build. Countries in green see better performance for this feature and build; countries in red see worse.

The analytics system was internally deployed, and was wired up for four different internal online services as a core telemetry tool. Those four teams used it to guide and manage their release process. Core features from this tool were incorporated into its successors, which are now part of the next generation of internal telemetry management systems.

Conclusion

This design remained close to both the data and the customers throughout. As we worked our way through the operationalization, making our questions more and more specific, we were able to figure out what visualizations would best address the questions. Sketching data often helped clarify the questions and also helped to identify edge cases and considerations we hadn't thought about before.

This process used all the tools of the data counseling process: interviews with users of the system to understand their interpretations of the data, sketches of ideas for interfaces, and plots of the data itself. These sketches, diagrams, and ideas enabled us to create a tool that allowed product teams to understand their deployed programs.

Acknowledgments

Danyel is grateful to Jacqueline Richards and Brian Bussone for helping to reconstruct the process we used, finding notes and prototypes, and their feedback on this chapter. We received additional feedback and encouragement from Ross Smith.

Further Reading

The Lync study, including the context around the data science aspects, is documented in Musson, Robert et al., "Leveraging the Crowd: How 48,000 Users Helped Improve Lync Performance." (*http://bit.ly/2nFQHKP*) *IEEE Software* 30 (2013): 38–45.

CHAPTER 8

Case Study 2: Visualizing Biological Data

Chapter 7 described a fairly straightforward case of a business intelligence challenge. This chapter chooses a somewhat more complex example from a very different domain. The question in this scenario was a challenge to operationalize: it required substantial scientific background. The complex scientific data meant that both the meaning and use of the data required more technical context and collaboration to operationalize.

This project was a collaboration with a team of biologists, led by Prof. Angela DePace at the Harvard Medical School. Miriah and her colleagues worked with this group for two years. During that time Miriah carried out a series of data counseling interviews, getting to know the ways that the biologists approached their data. In the process she developed a series of visualization prototypes, and the scientists used the prototypes to progressively refine their operationalization. These prototypes initially helped Miriah to understand the problem, then later to help shape the biologists' analysis. The final version became a vital component of the group's analysis pipeline.

This chapter illustrates how the techniques presented in Chapter 6 allowed the scientists to organize their data and to make sense of how a multitude of attributes relate to each other. The result used various design patterns (overview+detail, small multiples, interactive multiform views, and overlays) to give the scientists a detailed, intensive understanding of their data. In the course of building prototypes, the scientists realized that there were more ways to analyze their data than they had expected. The visualization tool allowed them not only to learn new things about their data but to think about their analysis differently.

This chapter simplifies the process, and leaves out some of the data counseling iterations in order to make the case study reasonable in length and scope. A fuller description can be found in an academic paper about the project (see "Further Reading" on page 139).

Background

The DePace Lab focuses on developmental biology, and is particularly interested in understanding how genes influence the physical features of animals. The scientists there are studying a set of fundamental *toolkit* genes—genes that are shared across many species, from flies to cats to apes to humans, and control the development of body parts in developing embryos. What is remarkable about these genes is that they are nearly the same in many species, and yet these species are physically very different. For example, the genes that control the development of eyes are very similar across a wide range of species even though a human's eyes are different from a cat's eyes, or a fly's.

A grand challenge in biology is understanding how these sets of similar genes produce such different results. Biologists know that differences between species are related to when and where these genes are turned on and off in developing embryos. What they do not yet understand is how these differences relate to physical traits or how these differences are encoded in the genome. Shedding light on these questions is the focus of the DePace Lab.

The scientists at the DePace Lab tackle these questions by studying fruit flies. They measure which genes are turned on or off, or more specifically, *how much* genes are on or off—called gene expression— in developing fruit fly embryos. Their data consists of gene expression measurements for about 50 genes, measured at 6 time points for every cell in an embryo. They are collecting this data for multiple different species of flies. By comparing the data across the different species, the lab hopes to link differences in gene expression to differences in physical features.

Setting the Context

The project began when a mutual colleague connected Miriah and Angela DePace. Angela was in the process of running experiments and collecting data, and was looking for new ways to analyze and compare datasets. A lunch meeting turned into a tour of the DePace Lab, followed by a series of informal interviews with members of the lab that included walkthroughs of their data analysis pipeline.

The group were already creating static visualizations in MATLAB to examine their data. They were overwhelmed with those first plots: dozens of variations of parameters looking at multiple types of data. There were too many different plots to understand, and they hoped Miriah could help them organize the way they thought about the data. Miriah rolled up her sleeves and took a look.

The researchers were comparing datasets—the gene expression measurements for different embryos—by trying to find cells in one embryo that had significantly different gene expression from cells in another embryo. They had developed an algorithm for finding these so-called *outlier cells*.

To analyze where the resulting outliers turned up in a particular embryo, the group visualized the data using a flattened, 2D representation of the embryo. The representation was created by mapping each cell in the football-shaped embryo to a 2D map where the head cells are on the left, tails cells on the right, and the back down the middle with the belly split along the top and bottom.

While the most natural representation of the data might seem to be a 3D view, the group preferred these 2D views because it was easier to quickly get a gist of the data than it was with a 3D representation that required interaction to spin the embryo around to see all sides. Figure 8-1 shows the cells represented as a 3D embryo at the top, and the flattened, 2D representation is at the bottom.

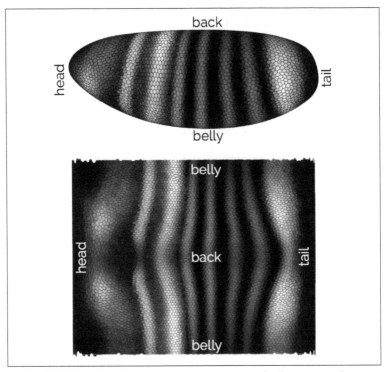

Figure 8-1. The top image shows the locations of cells in an embryo in a 3D view. The cells are colored here according an associated gene expression value. The bottom image shows the same embryo as a flattened, 2D view: head at the left, tail on the right; the belly wraps on the top and bottom edges. The images were generated using the PointCloudXplore (http://bit.ly/2j2Rns8) visualization software.

In Figure 8-2, the locations of the outliers from one embryo are shown using the 2D representation. The first thing to notice is that the outliers appear to cluster in regions as opposed to being scattered randomly. This was interesting to the biologists because cells that are spatially near each other are likely to have similar gene expression—a clustering algorithm found this to be true. The clusters are visually encoded using shape and color: all the pink triangle outliers are similar to each other, the blue circles are similar, and so on. The implication of this similarity is that whole groups of cells in one embryo could be significantly different from cells in another embryo.

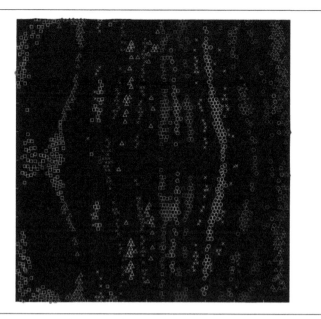

Figure 8-2. A visualization of outlier cells in an embryo using the 2D representation. Each point—either black or encoded with color+shape —is a single outlier cell. Each combination of color+shape is a clustered group, so all the teal circles or the pink triangles are in one group. Image courtesy of Angela DePace.

Zooming in a Level

Next, the biologists wanted to understand more specifically which genes were different in the outlier cells. In this project, a cell is characterized by a number of genes, which are measured at a number of different time points.

They created heatmap visualizations like the one shown in Figure 8-3 to examine the gene expression data of the outliers. The heatmap encodes gene expression values using color. Each column corresponds to a single cell, and the rows are time points and genes. Grouped columns correspond to the clusters of cells in the outlier cell plot in Figure 8-2, such as the pink triangles and teal circles. This visualization allowed the biologists to characterize the clusters of cells based on the patterns of gene expression. For example, all cells in group *bx*—the third column, which corresponds to the blue x's—are expressed fairly strongly at every time point for the *fkh* gene.

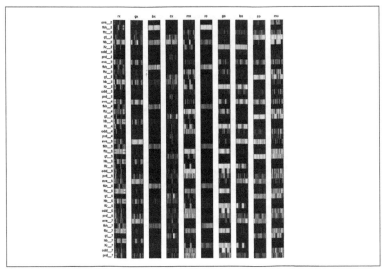

Figure 8-3. Small-multiples display of the outlier cells' gene expression measurements partitioned by the cluster groups. Clusters of cells are the columns; genes + time points are the rows. This view is linked to Figure 8-2 through labels: the blue circles correspond to the column bo and the blue x's to the column bx. Image courtesy of Angela DePace.

Characterizing the gene expression of each cluster was just one part of the solution; however, the biologists also needed to be able to characterize how this gene expression is *different* from the corresponding cells in another embryo. For each cell in the heatmap, they would create a corresponding heatmap, visualizing the gene expression data for the most similar cells in the other embryo. The result was hundreds of heatmaps. The group was overwhelmed and had trouble making sense of the pile of data.

Starting from Existing Material

It is common for groups to have created visualizations that address some of the challenges they face. Understanding why these existing artifacts were created and where their limitations are can be an invaluable part of the data counseling process. In this case, the fact that the team was hitting a wall in organizing the mass of visualizations they had created was a good indication that a more nuanced, bespoke solution was in order.

Improving the Existing Approach

We spent some time watching the scientists working with their visualizations and trying to understand what made this process difficult. We designed our first prototype to overcome the challenge of having to compare hundreds of heatmaps.

We observed that the scientists would use the 2D outlier cell view to ground their analysis of the heatmaps. For each cluster of cells in the 2D view, they would examine the corresponding set of heatmaps. This would entail flipping between the sheets of paper that represented the different heatmaps. This task of orientation—"what point in visualization 2 corresponds to this point in visualization 1?"— suggests an MLV design pattern that links two views together via user interaction. We wanted to reduce the feeling of being overwhelmed by the sheer volume of comparisons they were doing, which suggested an overview+detail design pattern that allows a user to get details on demand. The fact that the scientists would refer back to the 2D view (Figure 8-2) suggested that this visualization would make a great overview.

We built our first software prototype in Processing (*https:// www.processing.org*). This prototype, shown in Figure 8-4, is an MLV system consisting of both a multiform component and an overview+detail component. The left two views represent different views of the overall data. The leftmost is a heatmap that shows the gene expression values for all of the outlier cells, again partitioned based on the clustered sets of outliers; the middle view shows the spatial position in 2D of the outlier cells within the context of the complete set of embryo cells. Selecting a cluster in the heatmap highlights the associated cells in the spatial view. The middle view also serves as an overview of the data, where individual cells can be selected, causing expression profile details about those cells to be shown in the rightmost detail view. This detail view additionally shows a heatmap of the corresponding cells against which the selected cell was compared.

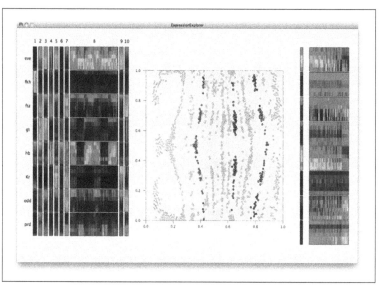

Figure 8-4. Screenshot of the first interactive software prototype we created. This tool used both the multiform and overview+detail design patterns for linked views. A video of this prototype in action can be found at the book's website (http://bit.ly/2jMnZm5).

In short, the prototype used the group's existing visualizations but replaced the manual look-ups between multiple sheets of paper with interactivity in software.

We deployed this prototype to the group. Three of the lab members integrated it into their data analysis workflow, replacing their use of the static plots with the new tool. After a week of use, we went back and conducted several contextual interviews with the group to understand how the interactivity impacted their analysis and under-standing. The interviews revealed that the tool allowed them study individual outlier cells in detail and easily compare an outlier to the set of corresponding cells in order to understand what differences in the gene expression patterns exist. These capabilities led the group to come to the conclusion that the outlier detection algorithm was too restrictive, resulting in a rethinking of their computational approach.

Similarity, Not Outliers

We had to revisit the operationalization. Instead of using an outlier detection algorithm to understand how the embryos differed, the group decided on a looser approach that simply characterized how similar each cell in one embryo was compared to corresponding cells in the other embryo. The task then became finding cells with low similarity. We updated the overview in the middle of the prototype to show a measure of similarity (our interestingness measure) for every cell in the embryo—an example of this view is shown in Figure 8-5. This similarity was computed from comparisons with the set of corresponding cells in the comparison embryo. This color-coding helped the group to locate the cells that were most different and to view the details of those cells on demand.

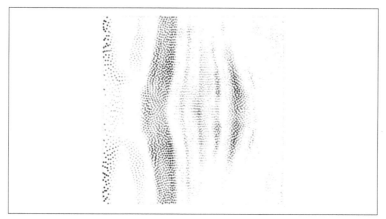

Figure 8-5. An updated 2D view of all the cells in an embryo; each cell is now color-coded by how similar it is to the most similar nearby cell in the other embryo. This visualization shows patterns of similarity and dissimilarity across the embryo.

The refined prototype let the group quickly explore many more different cells than the first version, and led them to make some interesting biological observations. Their exploration also highlighted that the experimental measurements from one of the species was plagued with low-level noise, causing the biologists to go back and modify their experimental procedures and recapture the data.

Visualization for Debugging Data

The situation described here is not unusual. Almost every experience we have had with visualization has involved discovering challenges in the data available and errors in the data collection and cleaning process, and forcing us to reconsider the operationalization. This is a healthy process—and a strong argument for getting to the data as soon as possible.

Using this prototype, the group began asking new questions of their data: what would a different similarity metric reveal? Could a different measure other than gene expression similarity help find cells of interest? How would their understanding change if they were to compare across multiple embryos?

In short, the interactive visualization caused the biologists to brainstorm about many new types of questions. The design of the tool, namely the overview+detail components, guided the group's framing of these questions in terms of using a metric to guide the investigation into a set of cells of interest.

A Final Version

We now knew that we would want to let the biologists play with different ways to compute similarity. We wanted to increase the flexibility of the tool and to allow the group to continue to expand the questions they wanted to answer.

We also wanted to revisit the visualizations themselves and apply good visualization design principles. One of the first changes we proposed to the group was to move away from using color to encode the gene expression measurements. Instead, we suggested using a specific temporal visualization to express the six time points for each gene.

Thus, we moved away from a heatmap view for a single cell's gene expression measurements:

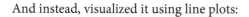

And instead, visualized it using line plots:

To compare gene expression across multiple cells, we created a small-multiples visualization of the line plots, which we call a *curve-map*. In the curvemap shown in Figure 8-6, we partitioned the data by gene along the columns, and by cells along the rows. This small-multiples view allowed us to stack up a set of line plots for user-selected cells that a user can quickly scan down, for each gene, to look for detailed differences between the cells.

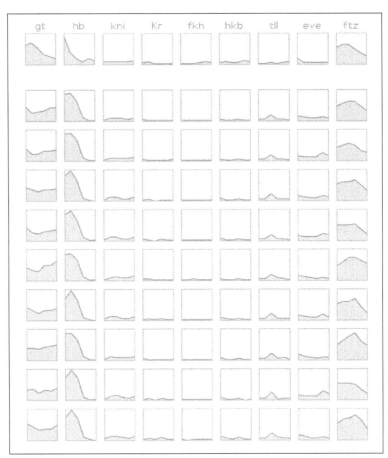

Figure 8-6. A curvemap of data, where the rows are cells and the columns are genes. The topmost row is a user-selected cell of interest, with the rest of the rows showing data for comparison cells. Scanning down the columns shows that the gt gene values are noticeably different over time in the comparison cells, while the ftz gene looks much more similar.

This visualization was a big change. The group initially resisted the new way of looking at the gene expression values; they were accustomed to the color-based heatmap. Once we showed them mockups of the new visualization using the group's *actual data*, however, they agreed that the new representation was easier to interpret.

It is important to sketch and prototype with actual data whenever possible in order to get buy-in from stakeholders, as well as to ensure that the real data does not break the design.

The new prototype again uses the overview+detail display from the original prototype to allow users to navigate to the cells they are most interested in studying in detail—only this time, the detail view is a curvemap (Figure 8-7). In this new tool, the scientist would select a cell in the 2D cell view; the system would then update the detailed view on the right to show that cell's gene expression along with the set of cells it corresponds to in the comparison embryo. A video of the tool in action can be found at the book's website (*http:// bit.ly/2BxP0kE*).

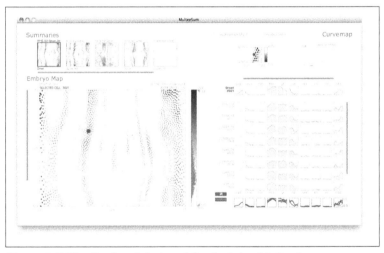

Figure 8-7. The final tool designed for the lab—MulteeSum—uses a variety of MLV patterns: overview+detail, small multiples, overlays, and multiform views. The tool also supports flexible upstream compu-tations of metrics that compare cells. A video of the tool in action can be found on the book's website (http://bit.ly/2BxP0kE).

It turned out to be difficult to scan through a vertical column of *many* line charts. In response to feedback from the biologists, we augmented the small multiples display with overlay plots at the bot-tom of each column. These overlays support direct comparison of the time curves and make it easy to see differences. For example, the *hb* gene curve expresses very differently in the test cell (shown in red) from its most similar neighbors (shown in black). These over-lays are important in the characterization of differences in when and where genes are expressed, which get back to the lab's high-level task.

This system supports the biologists in experimenting with different similarity metrics. The biologists can compute a variety of similarity metrics offline and load them all into the visualization tool. The tool takes in the multiple metrics and supports their investigation with another layer of overview that lets the biologist select a specific metric—this overview, in the upper left of the tool, is itself another small multiples display of available similarity metrics.

We created this interactive prototype in Processing and deployed it, along with a specification for a generic file format to support the upstream similarity computations, to the group. We followed up with the lab several weeks after deployment. The resulting tool supported a much broader set of analysis goals than we had initially imagined at the start of the collaboration, and is now one of the primary tools used by the DePace Lab as they analyze their data and continue their biological analysis.

Conclusion

The success of this project can be traced to several strategies. First, we needed to acquire a relatively deep understanding of the problem domain of the lab before we could actually understand how to build better tools. Interviews and observations got us part of the way there, but actually digging into the data by building a prototype helped in solidifying our understanding of the tasks the group were doing, and needed to do.

Second, we were able to get started by beginning with the existing visualization approach and searching for places where it ran into challenges. In this case, we took the existing views the group were creating and made them interactive.

The process of visualization taught the biologists more about the work they were carrying out than simply making sense of the data at hand. Only after we had built a visualization centered on outliers did they realize that outliers were an insufficiently general proxy to help them address their questions. Seeing their data in a new way led to a reformulation of the questions they were asking in the first place. It also identified significant errors in the data that they went back and corrected through new experimental procedures.

There is always a tension between the desire to maintain familiar visual patterns and the possibility that rejecting them will illuminate new issues. Our design maintained the 2D layout of cells, for example. On the other hand, changing from a heatmap to a curvemap helped clarify the different gene patterns and allowed the biologists to visually cluster genes together.

And finally, although not explicitly covered in this summary of the project, we iterated with the lab with many lo-fi prototypes, from sketches to mock-ups in Illustrator. The software prototypes were also developed with a throwaway mentality that let us avoid getting bogged down in implementation details and instead focus on getting our ideas into the hands of our users quickly. We found that it was important to present new ideas to the group with their own data, such as the shift from heatmaps to curvemaps. This allowed the group to engage with ideas as they would in their daily workflow, as well as allowing us to ensure that the real data would not break our design ideas. Watching the videos of our first interactive version and the final one, available at the book's website (*http://bit.ly/2BxP0kE*), gives a sense of how the technology changed over the course of the collaboration.

Further Reading

Figures 8-2 and 8-3 courtesy of Angela DePace.

The tool discussed in this chapter (*http://www.cs.utah.edu/~miriah/multeesum/*) is described in an academic paper: see Meyer, Miriah et al., "MulteeSum: A Tool for Comparative Spatial and Temporal Gene Expression Data." *IEEE Transactions on Visualization and Computer Graphics* 16 (2010): 908–917.

The biologists' research is described in Fowlkes, Charless et al., "A Conserved Developmental Patterning Network Produces Quantitatively Different Output in Multiple Species of Drosphila." *PLoS Genetics* 7 (2011): e1002346.

CHAPTER 9
Conclusions

Data visualization is a powerful way to make sense of the world, to share ideas with other people, and to help us understand what hidden meanings lie in our data. The skill of visualization is in finding ways to figure out what questions can be asked of the dataset, and what visual mappings will support answering those questions.

Creating effective visualizations is a process that entails working closely with a variety of stakeholders. It means gaining an understanding of where the data comes from and how it works, from the people who own or create it. It means learning what is being done with the data now, and what decisions are going to be made with it, from the people who are making those decisions. It means getting to know how users ultimately mean to interpret the data.

Creating effective visualizations also requires mapping questions to data, and data to visualizations. These mappings develop through many iterations of sketches and data-driven prototypes that let analysts see, as quickly as possible, what their data means and how they can interpret it. Sometimes the result is an interactive system of complex multiple linked views, and sometimes it requires just loading the data into an off-the-shelf tool.

Experiencing moments when meaning emerges from data can be incredibly exciting. These moments—when clients furrow their brows and say, "That's odd, I need to know more about that"—are what drive our work.

We hope this book will drive your excitement, too.

—Danyel Fisher, Seattle, Washington
Miriah Meyer, Salt Lake City, Utah
December, 2017

Index

Symbols
3D data, 60
  visualization in fruit flies case
    study, 127

A
actionable tasks, 24
actions, 18, 52-53
  action keywords cueing which vis-
    ualization to use, 53
  frequently encountered, 52
  verbs stakeholders use when dis-
    cussing data, 34
adjacency matrices, 76
analysts, 31
area charts, 72
attributes
  comparing in overlays, 99
  comparison in scatterplot matri-
    ces, 91
  comparison of subsets of data
    across, in small multiples, 89
  examining how an attribute varies
    continuously, 72
  of items, examining relationship
    between, 70
axes, alignment in multiple visualizations, 100

B
bar charts, 91
  comparing multiple groups, 66

in multiple linked views, interaction techniques, 102
learning resources for, 83
notched bar chart for software
  evolution in Lync case study,
  122
stacked and clustered bar charts
  comparing Lync distributions,
  114
bean plots, 64
Bing Maps, 5
binning, 50
  in quantitative histogram, 62
biological data, visualizing (see visualizing biological data, case study)
box plots, 64
brushing and linking (interaction
  technique), 97, 102

C
cardinality, reducing for categorical
  data, 50
case studies
  visualizing biological data,
    125-139
  visualizing telemetry to improve
    software, 107-124
categorical data, 48, 58
  histogram of, 61
  reducing cardinality for, 50
  transformations between ordinal
    data and, 49
charts

heatmaps and, 69
scatterplots vs., 66
dependent variables, 46
design spaces versus data space, 38
designing effective visualizations, 1-8,
141
deciding where visualization is
useful, 7
Hotmap, making decisions with
data, 3
process of, 3
detail views, 93
comparing versions in final UI of
Lync case study, 120
dimensions and measures, 46-52
dimensionality reduction and
clustering, 51
dimensions in ITIC example, 47
example, International Towing &
Ice Cream (ITIC), 46
transforming between dimension
types, 49
types of data, 48
domain expertise, bringing into the
operationalization process, 30
dotplot maps, 80
drilldowns, 50
durations, 49

E

encoding channels, 59
shared, in major visualization
types, 82
Excel, 37, 42
no pivoting data with, 51
exploratory data analysis (EDA), 22
exploring data (see data exploration)

F

feedback
eliciting on prototypes, 42
getting on proxies, explorations,
and visualization designs, 30
fruitfly case study (see visualizing
biological data, case study)

G

gatekeepers, 31
genetic data
exploring in overview+detail, 94
visualizing, 126
(see also visualizing biological
data, case study)
learning resoures for, 139
geographical visualizations, 80
comparing performance by country in Lync case study, 122
geospatial and temporal data, 99
ggplot, 91
Google Sheets, 42
The Grammar of Graphics, 91
groupings (or partitions), 17
groups
comparing multiple groups, 66-69
individual items in, visualizing
with scatterplots, 70

H

hairballs, 75
heatmaps, 4, 69
limitations of, 69
of outlier cells' gene expressions
in fruit flies case study, 129
hierarchies, 73
(see also networks or hierarchies)
depiction in tree views, 77
relative sizes of objects in, examining with treemaps and sunburst plots, 79
high-fidelity (hi-fi) prototypes, 41
histograms
categorical, 61
of performance data in Lync case
study, 112
quantitative, 62
smoothed, 63
Hotmap, 3, 37

I

independent and dependent variables, 46
insight, getting to, 1, 2
interactions, linked-view, 101, 103

operationalization, 9-27
    deciding how specific the process
        becomes, 24
    example, identifying good movie
        directors, 10
        exploring different definitions,
            22
    in telemetry visualization case
        study, refining the goal, 110
    linking the question to user need,
        82
    making a question concrete, 11
    making use of results, 25
    multiple linked views and, 103
    of best director question, 13
    repeating, 43
    tasks leading to new questions, 21
    techniques for supporting, 43
    well-operationalized tasks, 26
ordinal data, 48, 58
    transformations between categori-
        cal data and, 49
    transformations between continu-
        ous data and, 50
    transforming continous data into,
        using binning, 62
outlier cells, 127
    identifying similarity of cells
        instead of outliers, 133
    understanding more specifically
        genetic differences in, 129
    visualizations in 2D and 3D, 127
overlays, 87, 99
overview+detail visualizations, 87, 92
    detail views comparing versions
        in Lync case study, 120
    in fruit flies case study, 137
    in software prototype for fruit
        flies case study, 131
    in the operationalization process,
        103

P

Pandas, 37, 51
parts of a whole, demonstrating in
    pie charts, 68
perceptual concepts, 59
    colors in visualizations, 60

hierarchy of accuracy in compari-
    sons, 59
lines in visualizations, 60
three-dimensional data, 60
pie charts, 68
pivot tables, 51
pivoting data, 51
PowerBI, 42, 51
probability distribution function, 63
Processing, 37
    interactive prototype for fruit flies
        study, 138
product (in ITIC data), 47
prototypes, 29
    (see also rapid prototyping)
    fast-and-loose, getting ideas going
        with, 37
    range of, 38
proxies, 12
    need for a more refined proxy,
        identifying in a question or
        task, 17
    need to make decisions about, 26
    refining goal with, in telemetry
        visualization case study, 109
    software responsiveness in tele-
        metry visualization case study,
        108

Q

quantitative data, 58
    (see also continuous data)
questions
    guided by operationalization pro-
        cess, 26
    interview questions for data coun-
        seling, 33
    making concrete, 11
        best directors question, 13
    making specific, in data counsel-
        ing interviews, 34
    refining and revealing new lines
        of inquiry, 21
    refining into tasks and breaking
        down the tasks, 17

well-operationalized, characteristics of, 26
telemetry visualization (see visualizing telemetry to improve software, case study)
temperature (in ITIC data), 47
temporal data, 49
    in overlays, 99
textual data, visualizing, 81
time, 49
    (see also temporal data)
time (in ITIC data), 47
toolkit genes, study of, 126
tree views, 77
treemaps, 60, 77
    heatmaps and, 69
trellis charts, 88

U

unstructured interviews, 32

V

values (proxy), 12
Vega, 37, 91
violin plots, 64
Virtual Earth, 4
visual encodings, deriving from interviews discussing data, 34
visualization tools
    allowing incorporation of custom visuals, 42
    creating your own, 37
    pivoting data in, 51
    to explore data, 37
visualization-specific languages, 37
visualizations
    components of, 45-53
        breakdown in Lync case study, 110
        dimensions and measures, 46-52
        examining actions, 52-53
    creating effective data visualizations, 141
    for debugging data, 134

in support of operationalization process, 25
making use of operationalization results, 25
questions and corresponding visualizations, 58
starting from existing material, 130
understanding, 3
visualizing biological data, case study, 125-139
    final version, 134
    identifying similarity of embryonic cells, not outliers, 133
    improving the existing approach, 131-132
    learning resources for, 139
    project background, 126
    setting the context, 127
    zooming in on the data, 129
visualizing telemetry to improve software, case study, 107-124
    comparing distributions to understand "better", 114-116
    data, 110
    determining how to compare builds, 111-114
    final UI for high-level goals, 120-124
        additional visualizations, 122
    learning resources for, 124
    multiple scenarios, 116
    project background, 108-110
    sketching performance dashboards, 117-120
voice recording of interviews, 35

W

weather maps, 99
website for this book, 56
whisker plots, 64
word clouds, 81

Z

zoom sliders, 5

About the Authors

Danyel Fisher is a senior researcher at Microsoft Research; his work centers on information and data visualization. His work focuses on how users can make use of visualization to better make sense of their data; his work supports data analysts, end users, and people who just happen to have had a lot of information dumped in their laps. His research perspective starts from a background in human-computer interaction. Danyel received his MS from UC Berkeley in 2000, and his PhD from UC Irvine in 2004.

Miriah Meyer is an assistant professor at the University of Utah, where she runs the Visualization Design Lab. Her work focuses on designing visualizations for researchers and scholars that help them make sense of complex data. Miriah has collaborated with experts in a broad range of fields, including biology, geography, and poetry. She earned a PhD from the University of Utah in 2008, and worked as a postdoctoral research fellow at Harvard University until 2011.

Colophon

The animal on the cover of *Making Data Visual* is the dwarf gourami (*Trichogaster lalius*). Native to South Asia, these omnivorous, freshwater fish are typically found near the surface of slow-moving water in streams and lakes. Dwarf gouramis grow to about 3.5 inches in length. Males are diagonally striped in red and blue with narrow, pointed dorsal fins, whereas females are silvery with larger, rounded fins.

Because of their labyrinth organ—an auxiliary breathing organ that allows them to utilize oxygen directly from the air—these fish can survive in poorly oxygenated water as long as they have access to the surface. Slow-moving and still water provide an opportunity for males to build "bubble nests" out of dead, floating plant matter, which hold up to 800 fertilized eggs at a time. Incubation is complete within one day, and three days after hatching, spawn are capable of swimming beyond the safety of the nest.

Many of the animals on O'Reilly covers are endangered; all of them are important to the world. To learn more about how you can help, go to *animals.oreilly.com*.

The cover image is from *The Brockhaus Enzyklopädie.* The cover fonts are URW Typewriter and Guardian Sans. The text font is Adobe Minion Pro; the heading font is Adobe Myriad Condensed; and the code font is Dalton Maag's Ubuntu Mono.

Learn from experts.
Find the answers you need.

Sign up for a **10-day free trial** to get **unlimited access** to all of the content on Safari, including Learning Paths, interactive tutorials, and curated playlists that draw from thousands of ebooks and training videos on a wide range of topics, including data, design, DevOps, management, business—and much more.

Start your free trial at:
oreilly.com/safari

(No credit card required.)

www.ingramcontent.com/pod-product-compliance
Ingram Content Group UK Ltd.
Pitfield, Milton Keynes, MK11 3LW, UK
UKHW020846030425
457052UK00003B/85